The shepherd's kalender: or, the citizen's and country man's daily companion: ... To which is added, the country man's almanack, ... The fourth edition, with additions.

J. S.

The shepherd's kalender: or, the citizen's and country man's daily companion: ... To which is added, the country man's almanack, ... The fourth edition, with additions.
J. S.
ESTCID: N023156
Reproduction from Harvard University Houghton Library
Preface signed: J. S. With three final advertisement pages.
London : printed for A. Bettesworth, and C. Hitch, at the Red-Lyon in Pater-Noster-Row; R. Ware, at the Sun and Bible in Amen-Corner; and J. Hodges, at the Looking-Glass on London-Bridge, [1735?].
[8],157,[3]p. : ill. ; 12°

ECCO

Eighteenth Century Collections Online Print Editions

Gale ECCO Print Editions

Relive history with *Eighteenth Century Collections Online*, now available in print for the independent historian and collector. This series includes the most significant English-language and foreign-language works printed in Great Britain during the eighteenth century, and is organized in seven different subject areas including literature and language; medicine, science, and technology; and religion and philosophy. The collection also includes thousands of important works from the Americas.

The eighteenth century has been called "The Age of Enlightenment." It was a period of rapid advance in print culture and publishing, in world exploration, and in the rapid growth of science and technology – all of which had a profound impact on the political and cultural landscape. At the end of the century the American Revolution, French Revolution and Industrial Revolution, perhaps three of the most significant events in modern history, set in motion developments that eventually dominated world political, economic, and social life.

In a groundbreaking effort, Gale initiated a revolution of its own: digitization of epic proportions to preserve these invaluable works in the largest online archive of its kind. Contributions from major world libraries constitute over 175,000 original printed works. Scanned images of the actual pages, rather than transcriptions, recreate the works ***as they first appeared.***

Now for the first time, these high-quality digital scans of original works are available via print-on-demand, making them readily accessible to libraries, students, independent scholars, and readers of all ages.

For our initial release we have created seven robust collections to form one the world's most comprehensive catalogs of 18th century works.

Initial Gale ECCO Print Editions collections include:

History and Geography
Rich in titles on English life and social history, this collection spans the world as it was known to eighteenth-century historians and explorers. Titles include a wealth of travel accounts and diaries, histories of nations from throughout the world, and maps and charts of a world that was still being discovered. Students of the War of American Independence will find fascinating accounts from the British side of conflict.

Social Science

Delve into what it was like to live during the eighteenth century by reading the first-hand accounts of everyday people, including city dwellers and farmers, businessmen and bankers, artisans and merchants, artists and their patrons, politicians and their constituents. Original texts make the American, French, and Industrial revolutions vividly contemporary.

Medicine, Science and Technology

Medical theory and practice of the 1700s developed rapidly, as is evidenced by the extensive collection, which includes descriptions of diseases, their conditions, and treatments. Books on science and technology, agriculture, military technology, natural philosophy, even cookbooks, are all contained here.

Literature and Language

Western literary study flows out of eighteenth-century works by Alexander Pope, Daniel Defoe, Henry Fielding, Frances Burney, Denis Diderot, Johann Gottfried Herder, Johann Wolfgang von Goethe, and others. Experience the birth of the modern novel, or compare the development of language using dictionaries and grammar discourses.

Religion and Philosophy

The Age of Enlightenment profoundly enriched religious and philosophical understanding and continues to influence present-day thinking. Works collected here include masterpieces by David Hume, Immanuel Kant, and Jean-Jacques Rousseau, as well as religious sermons and moral debates on the issues of the day, such as the slave trade. The Age of Reason saw conflict between Protestantism and Catholicism transformed into one between faith and logic -- a debate that continues in the twenty-first century.

Law and Reference

This collection reveals the history of English common law and Empire law in a vastly changing world of British expansion. Dominating the legal field is the *Commentaries of the Law of England* by Sir William Blackstone, which first appeared in 1765. Reference works such as almanacs and catalogues continue to educate us by revealing the day-to-day workings of society.

Fine Arts

The eighteenth-century fascination with Greek and Roman antiquity followed the systematic excavation of the ruins at Pompeii and Herculaneum in southern Italy; and after 1750 a neoclassical style dominated all artistic fields. The titles here trace developments in mostly English-language works on painting, sculpture, architecture, music, theater, and other disciplines. Instructional works on musical instruments, catalogs of art objects, comic operas, and more are also included.

The BiblioLife Network

This project was made possible in part by the BiblioLife Network (BLN), a project aimed at addressing some of the huge challenges facing book preservationists around the world. The BLN includes libraries, library networks, archives, subject matter experts, online communities and library service providers. We believe every book ever published should be available as a high-quality print reproduction; printed on-demand anywhere in the world. This insures the ongoing accessibility of the content and helps generate revenue for the libraries that work hard to preserve these important materials.

The following book is in the "public domain" and represents an authentic reproduction of the text as printed by the original publisher. While we have attempted to accurately maintain the integrity of the original work, there are sometimes problems with the original work or the micro-film from which the books were digitized. This can result in minor errors in reproduction. Possible imperfections include missing and blurred pages, poor pictures, markings and other reproduction issues beyond our control. Because this work is culturally important, we have made it available as part of our commitment to protecting, preserving, and promoting the world's literature.

GUIDE TO FOLD-OUTS MAPS and OVERSIZED IMAGES

The book you are reading was digitized from microfilm captured over the past thirty to forty years. Years after the creation of the original microfilm, the book was converted to digital files and made available in an online database.

In an online database, page images do not need to conform to the size restrictions found in a printed book. When converting these images back into a printed bound book, the page sizes are standardized in ways that maintain the detail of the original. For large images, such as fold-out maps, the original page image is split into two or more pages.

Guidelines used to determine how to split the page image follows:

- Some images are split vertically; large images require vertical and horizontal splits.
- For horizontal splits, the content is split left to right.
- For vertical splits, the content is split from top to bottom.
- For both vertical and horizontal splits, the image is processed from top left to bottom right.

Just Publish'd.

THE Instructor: Or, Young Man's best Companion Containing, Spelling, Reading, Writing, and Arithmetick in an easier Way than any yet published; and how to qualify any Person for Business, without the Help of a Master. Instructions to write Variety of Hands, with Copies both in Prose and Verse. How to write Letters on Business or Friendship. Forms and Indentures, Bonds, Bills of Sale, Receipts, Wills, Leases, Releases, &c. Also Merchants Accompts, and a short and easy Method of Shop and Book-keeping, with a Description of the Product, Counties, and Market-Towns in *England* and *Wales*. Together with the *Carpenter*'s plain and exact Rule: Shewing how to measure *Carpenpenters*, *Joyners*, *Sawyers*, *Bricklayers*, *Plaisters*, *Plummers*, *Masons*, *Glasiers*, and *Painters* Work How to undertake each Work, and at what Price; the Rates of each Commodity and the common Wages of Journeymen; with *Gunter*'s Line, and *Coggeshall*'s Description of the Sliding Rule Likewise the Practical Gauger made Easy, the Art of Dialling, and how to erect and fix any Dial, with Instructions for Dying Colouring, and making Colours; and some General Observations for Gardening every Month in the Year. To which is added The Family's best Companion, with Instructions for Marking on Linnen; how to Pickle and Preserve, to make diverse sorts of Wines, and many excellent Plaisters and Medicines, necessary in all Families By *George Fisher*, Accomptant. *London*. Printed for *A. Bettesworth*, and *C. Hitch* in *Pater-noster Row*; *R. Ware* in *Amen Corner*; and *J. Hodges* on *London-bridge*. Price 2 s. 6 d.

THE

Shepherd's Kalender:

OR, THE

Citizen's and *Country Man's*

Daily COMPANION:

Treating of many Things that are Useful and Profitable to Man kind, with above Two Hundred wonderful Curiosities never before Published Also, a Discourse of the *Eclipses* of the Sun and Moon, with Rules to know when they will happen Infallible Signs of the Weather To know when Wet or Dry, and when sudden Storms arises, hot or cold Weather, by living Creatures A curious Observation never made Publick before.

An Account of the Lucky and Unlucky Days throughout the Year The *Mosaick* Wand to find out hidden Treasures The Calculation of Nativities, and to resolve all Lawful Questions.

To which is Added,

The Country Man's Almanack, Directing when to Bleed, and Diet the Body: A Treatise of *Bees*, *Warrens*, ordering of *Cattle*, *Hawks*, and how to kill *Vermine*. The Measuring Land and Timber The Art of Ringing. The true Value, or Worth of a Single Penny Or, a Caution to keep Money.

Being above Forty Years Study and Experience of a Learned Shepherd.

The Fourth Edition, with Additions.

London Printed for *A. Bettesworth*, and *C Hitch*, at the *Red-Lyon* in *Pater-noster-Row*; *R. Ware*, at the *Sun* and *Bible* in *Amen-Corner*; and *J. Hodges*, at the *Looking-glass* on *London-bridge*.

F. 74. 1. 6

Just Publish'd.

Printed for James Hodges, *at the* Looking-glass *on* London-bridge *The Second Edition, Corrected and Amended, with large Additions.* Price 3 s

1. A Compleat Melody: Or, The Harmony of Sion. In Three Parts. Containing, 1. A new compleat Introduction to all the true Grounds of Music, both Vocal and Instrumental, by Way of Dialogue, in a new and easy Method. With an Explaration of all the usual Terms used in Music, collected from the *Greek*, *Latin*, *French*, *Italian*, &c. In Ten Chapters. 2. The Psalms of *David* new tun'd. Which Music expresses the true Sense and Sounds of the Words more than any ever yet publish'd. With an Alphabetical Table of all the Tunes, and what Psalms are proper to each Tune. Also a Table of Psalms suited to the Feasts and Fasts of the Church of *England*, and other Varieties of Life. With Fourteen *Gloria Patri's*, suited to the true Measure of every Psalm in the Book 3. A new and select Number of divine Hymns and easy Anthems on several Occasions, with several Canons of Two, Three, and Four Parts in one.

The whole is compos'd in Two, Three, and Four Musical Parts, according to the most authentick Rules, for Voice or Organ. By *William Tansur*, of *Ewell*, [near *Epsom*] in the County of *Surry*

Thro' all the changing Scenes of Life, in Trouble (and in Joy,
The Praises of my God shall still my Heart and (Tongue employ.
Psalm XXXIV. 1.

THE PREFACE TO THE READER.

Reader,

IN this Laboured Work *you will find so many Useful and Profitable Things, that I am persuaded to be Constrained to acknowledge, you never before found the like in any* (*of what Volume soever*) *and I have digested them into so Plain and Easie a Method, that any ordinary Capacity may Comprehend what has so long been handled in Ambiguous Sentences, Dark, and Abstruse, to keep all those that are very learned in Ignorance: As for the truth of what is here set down, in Relation to* Prognosticks *of what Weather, or any other Matters in the vast variety contained in this Book, a very long and large Experience has Confirmed it to me, so that, if I might speak in General Terms, I may truly say There is no Ground left for a Scruple: But not to Commend what must Infinitely Applaud itself, being so Universally useful, not for Limited Years, but all, or the greater part of it for ever, I shall only Presume to Affirm, it is the best of the kind that ever was Exposed to the World,*

World, and cannot but gain a general Esteem. It's true, it was mainly Calculated for the Meridian *of Rural Affairs, but contain so many different matters, that it cannot but be helpful to all sorts of People, of what Quality or Degree soever. As not only giving the True Account of Time, but moveable Feasts, likewise when the moveable Terms begins and ends, also the fixed Terms in like manner, with the Returns of every Term Eclipses, and the Nature of them · Remarkable Days (in relation to Weather) throughout the whole Year · Also as to Diseases in Man or Beast Scarcity and Plenty, &c. Days Lucky and Unlucky, to begin or do any Business on Signs of Weather in all particulars: Prodigies, Meteors, and Blazing-Stars what they Prognosticate, and what their Causes Rules for the Management of Husbandry for every Month in the Year: Signs of Diseases in Cattle, and how to prevent and Remedy them · The Curious Art of telling Good and Bad Fortune, by the Rules of Astrology: The whole Mystery of Love: And finding out Thieves that Rob you: Also to prevent affrightning Dreams and Fears in the Night · To Travail in Safety · How to tell any Number one shall think, be it never so great: To know the Planet that hath Dominion in the Nativity of any Person The Art of discovering the Truth from Falshood: How to know whether you shall be Successful in any matters you engage in against another: To know whether the Party you Love be Virtuous and Chaste · To prevent or take Vermin, that come to destroy Poultry or Coney Warrens. To know what Place is best to live and thrive in, whether one shall be rich or poor, long life or short, what Sickness, or Crosses shall befal one: The Universal Doctor or Astrological and Physical Observations on casting Urine, relating to health and sickness, with cautions to prevent threatning Evils: A Treatise of Bees, how to*

Order, Preserve, Swarm, Gather their Honey, and all other Matters relating to them: The Warreners Instructor, or a Treatise of Coneys, their ordering to Preserve or Encrease them. The Falconers choice Instructor, or the best way to Manage, Feed, Purge, Scour, and keep Hawks to fly at all sorts of Game, and to do whatever is requisite for their Preservation, Well ordering, and to make them expert in what they are designed for, or required to perform. A plain and easie Introduction to the most curious Art, and healthful Exercise of Ringing Musically on 3. 4. 5. 6. 7. 8. or 9. Bells. How a Country-Man may know how much Hay or Corn his Barn will hold before it be put into it. How to know the Measure that ought to be in Cords or Stacks of Wood, to tell what a Clock (when the Sun Shines) by Ones Hand: A Catalogue of the Markets, and the Days they are kept on in the several Counties and Shires in England and Wales. Also an exact Catalogue of the Fixed and Moveable Fairs held Yearly in England and Wales, the Days and time of their continuance: the like for Exactness never before Published: Likewise, a Table for reducing Pounds into Shillings, Pence, and Farthings, and the contrary. The true Value, or worth of a Single Penny. Or a caution to keep money, being a way to live happy in hard times. And many other Matters too tedious to be mentioned in a Preface: But more at large expressed in this Book. Which will give you such satisfaction, as you can in any Reason desire.

I need not (as I think in this Place) say any more in Commendation of this Book, but that you have in it, Profit and Pleasure united, and a more Useful one (of this kind) you cannot expect. For when you find any that Equals, or Exceeds it, You may conclude you found a Phœnix.

Therefore, Relying on the Merit of what is here Written, I shall Close with Recommending it to my Country-men *in general, and to Lovers of* Art, *and Critical Observations in particular; in which they may find the greatest* Mysteries *of* Art *and* Nature; *And such other* Matters *as are exceeding Edifying. So that (take it all together) it cannot but be wonderfully satisfactory to the* Reader: *As for me, I covet no Praise as many do:*

For he who Writes to get himself a Name,
In this dull Age, is indigent of Fame.

And so only sending it Abroad for the Benefit of all, I subscribe myself

Yours to serve YOU,

J. S.

Eliza Dalby

THE

THE Shepherd's Kalender, &c.

A Computation of Time, in Minutes, Hours, Days, Weeks, Months, Years, divided into Quarters, with Signs Governing; as also of the Planetory Dominions.

IT is not fit (in this usual Work) to Omit any thing that may prove profitable and advantageous to the *Reader*; and since the Exact knowing of Times and Seasons, is one main thing Requisit, I shall here set it down, not only for the present, but future Years, that (without the help of any other *Kalender*) it may be easily found out,

First then, The Measure of Time arises from Minutes, 60 of them make an Hour, 24 Hours a natural Day, &c 7 Days goes to a Week, 4 Weeks to a Month, 13 such *Lunar* Months, a Day, and 6 Hours to a Year, tho' the Year is commonly divided into 12 *Solar* Months, or for twelve Signs, which the Sun passes through, in the Circle of a Year; so that one Month carries more Days than another; as in this antient observing Verse is seen.

> *Thirty Days hath Fruit-bearing* September,
> *Moist* April, *Hot* June, *and cold* November:
> *Short* February *Twenty Eight alone*;
> *The other months, have either Thirty One*,
> *And* February, *when the Fourth Year's run*,
> *Do's gain a Day from the swift moving Sun*!

So that by this it is plain, that every fourth Year, called *Bissextile*, or *Leap Year*, there is allowed to *February* 29 Days

The Year again is divided into 4 Quarters, *viz*. The Feast of the *Annu*, or the Blessed Virgin *mary*, called *Lady-day*, *march* 25 from its beginning under the Signs of *Capricorn*, *Aquarius*, and *Pisces*: The next, the Feast of St. *John Baptist*, called *midsummer-day*, *June* 24 extending from the former, under the Signs of *Aries*, *Taurus*, and *Gemini*; the next Quarter, is the Feast of St *michael*, the Arch Angel, called *michaelmas day*, *September* 29 Extending from *midsummer*, under the Signs of *Cancer*, *Leo*, and *Virgo* The last Quarter-day, is the Feast of the *Nativity* of our Blessed *Saviour*, called *Christmas day*, *December* 25 Extending from *michaelmas*, under the Signs *Libra*, *Scorpio*, and *Saggitarius*; and these, as I shall hereafter shew, have great Influence, joined with the Seven Planets, *viz Sol*, *Luna*, *mars*, *mercury*, *Jupiter*, *Venus*, and *Saturn*; each of these latter, governing a several Day in the Week.

And now, because there are some Festival, and other Days, that are not fixed, but Vary, and fall

Higher

Higher and Lower according to the Change of the *Moon*, I shall shew you, without the help of a common *Kalender*, how you may find out on what days or times they fall out for ever.

To know what Month and Day the moveable Feasts and Terms will fall on for many Years to come.

THE next *Tuesday*, after the *New moon*, in *February*, is *Shrove Tuesday*, and the precedent *Sunday* is *Shrove Sunday*, let it fall out sooner or later in the *Month*; but if the *Moon* happen to Change on a *Tuesday*, *Shrove Tuesday* falls not on that Day, but on the *Tuesday* following, and sometimes, by Reason of their being no *New-Moon* or a very late one, it falls in *March*; but the Rule is the same.

The seventh *Sunday*, after *Shrove-Sunday*, is *Whitsunday*, and the *Thursdoy* next, save one, before *Whitsunday*, is *Ascension Day*, or *Holy Thursday* But to make it yet plainer, I shall give you a Table, how they fall out for several Years to come.

Year	*Shrove-sun*		*Easter day*		*Ascen. d*		*Whit-sun.*	
1706	*March*	6	*April*	2	*June*	2	*June*	12
07	*Febru.*	19	*April*	9	*May*	18	*May*	28
08	*Febru.*	11	*March*	13	*May*	9	*May*	19
09	*March*	2	*April*	20	*May*	29	*June*	8
10	*Febru.*	15	*April*	5	*May*	14	*May*	24
11	*Febru.*	7	*March*	28	*May*	6	*May*	16
☉	☾		♂		☿		♀	

And thus you may proceed to know, for a *Thousand*, or more Years to come. And now, because the *Terms* are two of them moveable, I shall

say

say but a little of the two fixed *Terms*; but of the other, I shall lay down Rules how they may be found out in any Year, with their Returns.

As for the fixed *Terms*, that called *Hillary Terms*, always begins the 23*d* of *Jan* and endeth the 12*th* or 13*th* of *Feb.* and hath four Returns, *viz Quin. Pas. Tre Quin. Pas Cras Pas.*

Michaelmas Term. is the other fixed *Term*, beginning the 24*th* of *Octo* and ends the 28*th.* of *Nov.* and hath six Returns, *viz Tres. mich mens. mich. Cras. An. Cras mar Octo mar Quin. mar.*

As for the two moveable *Terms*, they are *Trinity Term*, and *Easter Term*, *Easter Term* always begins 17 Days after *Easter* Day, and endeth the *Monday* after *Ascension* Day, and hath five Returns, *viz. Quin Pas. Tre Pas. mens. Pas. Quin. Pas. Cras Pas*

Trinity Term begins the *Friday* next after *Trinity Sunday*, and the *Wednesday* fortnight after it ends, and hath four Returns, *viz Cras. Tri. Octo. Tri Quin. Tri. Tre Tri* but of the falling out of the moveable *Terms*, to make it yet more plain I shall give a brief Table how they fall, for some Years to come

Year.	Easter Term		Trinity Term.	
	Begins	Ends	Begins	Ends
1706	May 11	June 6	June 24	July 13
07	April 26	May 22	June 6	June 25
08	April 17	May 13	May 31	June 1[illegible]
09	May 7	June 2	June 20	July 9
10	April 2[illegible]	May 18	June 5	June 24
11	April 14	May 10	May 25	June 16
12	May [illegible]	May 29	June 16	July 5
13	April 2[illegible]	May 21	June 8	June 27

And according to this Table, you may proceed

by the aforegoing Directions, to any Number of Years, which will be very useful to many Imergencies, this Book being the best of Kalenders, for all useful Directions, containing a great deal more than any, may serve the yearly Charge and Trouble of buying, and carrying about you any other, and by the way farther Note:

Eight Days before any *Term* begins, the *Exchequer* openeth, except *Trinity Term*, before which it opens four Days, and no more.

Eclipses of the Sun *and* Moon, *how caused with Rules to know when they will happen*

AS for the *Moons* being Eclipsed, it is when the *Earth* interposes (in a direct Line) between it, and the *Sun*: So that the shadow arises so high, as to reach the *Opacus*, or neither part of the *Moons Orb*, which only happens at a time or Opposition of a *Full Moon*, or a little before or after the *Full*, and this is when they are in the Sign of the *Dragons Head* or *Tail*, which is only the Infection of two Circles, *viz.* The Ecliptick, and the Diff rent which Circle, the *Moon* moves about in.

The Eclipse of the *Sun* is caused by the Interposition of the *Moon's* dark Body between us, & it: so that, till they depart from Oppositions, there is an Eclipse, more or less. But the *Sun* being far bigger than the *Moon*, cannot suffer a Total Eclipse, though the *moon* often does, because the Earth is bigger than the *moon*. and so the Shaddow many times totally covers it from the *Sun*, for a time

If the *moon* at the time of her true Opposition to the *Sun*, [illegible] be different from either of the

named

named points, less than to 10 Degrees, 21 Minutes, and 20 Seconds, then the *Moon* cannot avoid suffering an Eclipse.

If this *Latitude* of the *Moon*, at the time of a visible Conjunction, be less than 30 *Minutes*, 4 *Seconds*, she will Eclipse the *Sun*, but if the Apparent *Latitude* of the *Moon* exceed 40 *Minutes*, 5 *Seconds*, then can there be no Eclipse.

Therefore the apparent *Latitude*, being more than 30 *Minutes*, 40 *Seconds*, and less than 34 *Minutes*, 51 *Seconds*, then in all probability there will happen an Eclipse of the *Sun*, though not to a very great degree: And by the Rules at all times,

may

may the Eclipse be found out, as to the time of their happening; and to save your Eyes in gazing on the Sun Eclipsed, take the Image of it in a *Mirror*, or *Looking-Glass*, and by that means you may plainly see how the Eclipses Encreases, and Diminishes, &c.

Prognosticks, or Predictions, on the Days of the Week, that New Year's-Day *shall fall on; Relating to the Weather, to fall out, throughout the Year, Scarcity and Plenty: Diseases, that will happen to People, also to Cattle.*

MAny have considered the whole Year, upon the Day it enters on, *viz.* The first of *January*, being the *Circumcision Day* of our Savour, commonly called *New Year's-Day*, and many Things are drawn from it, throughout all the Months of the Year, as they fall out, or begin on this Day: So that being proper to my Matter, and a stress laid upon them, by many prudent People, knowing in this *Art* and *Science*, I shall give my Opinion or Judgment on them, from long Observation.

Observations on the Years entring on Sundays.

If *New Year's-Day* (the first of this Month) fall on a *Sunday*, it denotes, the rest of the Winter will be very cold and sharp, with Frosts; but of little continuance; the greater part moist, with cold Rains. *The Summer hot*, but pestered with violent Rains; yet not so often, but the Earth

Earth will kindly bring forth great Plenty of

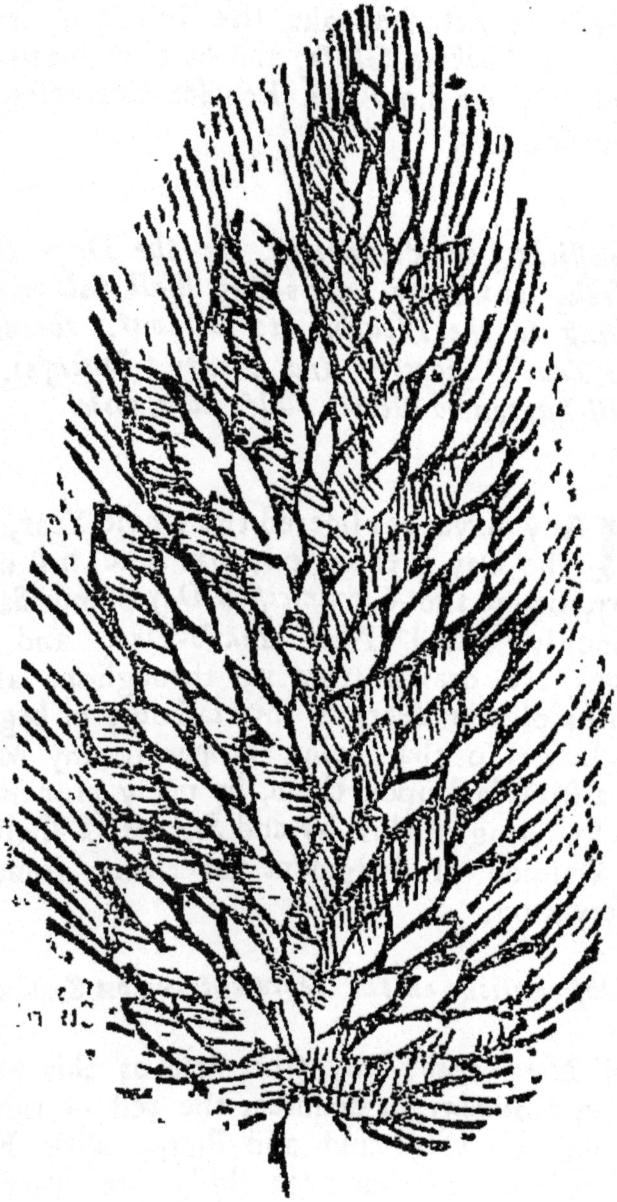

Corn, Roots, Herbs, and Fruits: Meat will be Cheap;

Cheap Among young People Fevers and Agues will be Rife And the greater number of those that die, will be of the younger Sort: For Cattle, it will be a healthy Year.

Observations on Monday.

If the Year enters on *Monday*, it is observed, that the Winter will be mild Not afflicted with sharp Frosts, or black Winds yet somewhat Rainy So that great overflowings shall happen, and much harm be done by Floods. The *Summer* however shall be temperate, but Blasts in the Spring: And Caterpillars (brought with the *East* Wind) much spoil the Fruits of the Earth: many Shipwrecks will be heard of, and some Great Men promoted to higher Dignities and Honours, for their good Services And this Year, more Women than Men will die, travailing in Child-birth, proving very fatal to many of them Pasture will be scarce Yet plenty of Corn, and Provisions reasonably cheap enough Griping of the Guts, if not the Bloody-Flux, and the Small-pox, will be very Rife.

Observations on the Year's entring on a Tuesday.

In this Case, the *winter* will be valuable the Weather often given to Change from Wet to Frost. Then to sleet and Snow Then Cloudy, open Weather. Sun-shine, and the like. So that the Frosts so happening, will be much prejudicial to the Fruits of the Earth, by reason of the often freezing the Snow water at the *Corn*, *Plants*, *Flowers*, *Herbage*, *Roots*, &c. As for the

the *Summer*, it will be hot and dry and scorching up tender Things, which will produce a scarcity of all Things, but Wheat and Barley; the Air will be thick and gross, because little Winds or Thunder will be stirring to purge it: So that many Diseases will (in all likelihood) happen, particularly the *Bloody Flux*; of which many will die.

Observations on the Year, beginning on a Wednesday.

The Year entering on this Day, produces a temperate *Winter*, yet somewhat wet and moist, though free from high boisterous Winds, some small matter of Snow and Frost, may be expected towards the latter end: The Spring, however, will produce much Grass, and the Corn spring up well: The *Summer* will be (for the most part) close, and cloudy Weather, hot, and sultry, making it sickly, subject to Fevers, Inflamations, and other hot Diseases, yet Handy crafts, and Husband men, shall gain Riches, and Trading flourish more than at other times, here will be breakings-out, blains, blotches, and boils on Cattle; and many die: So that Flesh will be dear, but to make amends, Corn cheap

Observations on the Year, beginning on Thursdays.

This produces a long *Winter*, mostly dry, with cold Winds, yet wholsome and healthy. The *Summer* (a great part of it) temperate, though (in Harvest-time) much Rain will fall, with Thunder and Lightning, doing much mischief (by the over-flowing of the Rivers, and Land-floods) to the Corn,

Corn, yet there will be no want of Plenty: murmourings, and discontent will be among some People, and mischief ensue thereon. People much given up to Vice, particularly that of Whoredom: Taxes will decrease, and Trade revive: For the most part, the Season will be healthful, but many troubled with Catarrs, Asthmas, and Consumptive Coughs, in the fall of the Leaf, and most part of the *Winter*, to their no small Affliction, yet fewer die, than the last Year.

Observations on the Year, beginning on a Friday.

If the first Day of *January* happen on a *Friday*, expect the *winter* dry, for the most part, many *black Frosts*, but of no long Continuance; the *winds* blowing moderately, will so Purge the Air, that will prove very Healthful, but the *Spring* coming in Wet, it will be but an indifferent *Harvest-time*; yet *Grass Garden*, and *Orchard Fruits*, shall 'scape tolerably well, but poor People will be in Need, and much Distress, for want of *Employment*, Diseases in the Eyes will be very Rife, as also the spotted Fever, Calentures: Cattle will likewise be Diseased, and many Die, making Flesh dear.

Lastly, Observations on the Years, beginning on a Saturday.

New Year's-Day, falling on a *Saturday*, the *winter* will be pretty moderate, though accompanied with Frosts, but not extream in holding long at a time, yet the frequent Thaws, and Free-

zing

zing ſuddenly upon it, will do more hurt than if it had held However, the Earth mellowed by this, will produce a fruitful *Summer*, ſo that there will be good ſtore of Corn, and other Fruits, and much Fodder for Cattle ſo that Fleſh will be Cheap The Diſeaſes this Year, will much fall on aged People, ſo that many will die, more than uſual, in other Years Tertian Fevers will be very Rife, many Robberies, and other Outrages will be committed in the Face of the Sun, ſome Murmurings, and Repinings, will happen, but not to any effect.

Thus, *Reader*, have I given you *Prognoſticks* for the Year, from the Day it begins, very Remarkable among the Learned and Wiſe *men* of the *Caldeans*, *Arabians*, *Ægyptians*, and many *Europeans*, leaving the Event to take Effect, from your making Remarks on what has been hinted, as you find it come to paſs. I proceed now to other matters of Moment.

Unlucky Days in every month, Dangerous to begin any Buſineſs on, Fall ſick, Bleed, Purge, Journey, &c

THE Obſervation of the Antient Phyſicians and Aſtrologers, have found out (by long Experience) that many Days, by the malevolent Effects of the Planets, they have proved dangerous to Men, Women, and Children, and, therefore, to Caution them (from Enterprizing any thing of moment on them) have ſet them down in their Order, as followeth

In *January* are eight Days, which ought to be avoided, and theſe are they, 1. 2 4 5 10 15 17. and the 19.

In

In *February* only 3. *viz.* the 8 9. 17
In *March* 3 *viz* the 15 16 21
In *April* there are only 2 *viz* the 15. and 21.
In *May* there are 3 *viz* the 7. 15. and 20.
In *June* there are but 2 bad Days, *viz.* 4. 7.
In *July* 2 *viz* 15 and 20. Days
In *August* there are 2 unlucky Days, 19 and 20.
In *September* there are 2. *viz.* the 6 and 7.
In *October* there is but 1 *viz.* the 6 Day.
In *November* there are 2. *viz.* 5 19.
In *December* there are 5 *viz* the 6 7. 11. 15. 16.

The *Canicular*, or *Dog days*, are ever held perilous, to fall Sick, to Bleed, take Physick in, or take too much Love-Posset between the Sheets, over-heat one self with Labour, Travel, or the like. These begin the 19th Day of *July*, and continue to the 28th Day of *August*

As for the other Days (not mentioned as bad Days) proceed in your Affairs, and prosper, but, on any of the Ominous Days, to fall Sick, is a Sign of a doubtful Recovery, if at all, and those take a long Journey, beginning it on any one of them, will be in Danger to fall Sick, or get some great hurt by the Way, if not die, and never return Home. Whosoever weddeth a Wife on any of these Days, will find Sorrow and Crosses in such a Wedlock, if not be forced to part in a little time; any great Work begun, will not prosper, nor come happily to an End, as expected.

The most remarkable Days in the Year, that are accounted Fortunate, to begin any weighty Matter on.

Since the Antients have layed great stress, as well upon the *Lucky* Days, as the *Unlucky*, it it will be convenient to place them in Order one, after another, and Note (by the way) that the I ſhall name but ſome few, as exceeding *Lucky* Days for *Marriage Bargains* going a *Journey*, or beginning a *Voyage* : And what every elſe is of weight and moment : Yet all the reſt, not *marked* before to be *Unlucky*, in each *Month*, are indifferent *Lucky*, and not to be Neglected, when your Occaſions require you to imploy them, leſt you be either taxed with *ſloath*, or *ſuperſtition*, in *Time* and *Seaſons*.

Lucky Days, &c.

Twelfth-Day, or *Epiphany*, —— ——*January* 6
The Converſion of St. *Paul*. ——— *January* 25
The Purification of the Virgin *Mary*, ——*Febr.* 2
Valentine's day, ——————————— *Febr* 14
The Annun or the Virgin *Mary*,———*March* 25
St. *Mark* the Evargeliſt,———————*Apr* 25
St. *Philip* and *Jacob*,————————*May* 1
St. *Barnabas*, or the longeſt Day,—— ——*June* 11
St. *John* Baptiſt, ——— ——————*June* 24
St. *Peter* the Apoſtle, —————————*June* 29
St *James*'s Day, ————————— ——*July* 25
St. *Bartholomew*'s Day, ——————— *Aug.* 24
St. *michael*'s Day,————————*September* 29
St. *Luke*'s Day, ——————————*Octo.* 18
St. *Simon* and *Jude*'s Day, ——— ———*Octo* 28
All Saints, ————————————— *Nov.* 1
St *Andrew*'s Day, ——————————*Nov* 30
St. *Thomas*'s Day, —— ——————*Dec* 21
Christmas-day, —————— ——————*Dec.* 25
St *Stephen*'s Day, ————————————*Dec.* 26
St *John* the Evangeliſt ——— ——————*Dec.* 27

Theſe are look'd on as Days that brings Bleſſings with them, yet, over and above.

Ordinary

Ordinary Days throughout the Year, more successful than others, not Named, already for Lucky Days.

IN *January* are 3 more particular happy Days, *beside what I named*, though the Rest not *marked ill* (as I have said) are *successful* enough, *viz.* the 16. 18. 26.

In *February* there are 4 *viz.* 10 19 27. 28.
In *March* there are 2. *viz.* 14. 18.
In *April* there are 3 *viz.* 13 22. 27
In *May* there are 5 *viz* 3. 5. 7 11. 19.
In *June* there are 4. *viz.* 10. 17. 20 27.
In *July* there are 6. *viz.* 1. 13. 19. 21 27. 30.
In *August* there are 3 *viz* 3 7. 9.
In *September* there are 5 *viz* 4 8 11. 15 19.
In *October* there are 3 *viz* 1 8 13.
In *November* there are 4 *viz* 3 9 11 15.
In *December* there are 3 *viz* 9 13 17.

And on these Days (favoured by the more immediate Influence of the Plants) many Wonderful Action, and Things have been done, to an accomplished Success, as well by the mighty of the World, as the Ordinary Sort Insomuch, that they have been Celebrated by the Antients, and Festivals appointed on them with *songs*, in praise of what great *Atchievements* have been done on them And these Festivals Promulged only for the sake of the *Good Luck* these Days prodnce: but let me tell you by the bye, however, that if you undertake any unlawful Enterprize, it will not prosper on these Days; Therefore, let your Designs be good, and fear

not

not the Succeſs to your Wiſh according to this Prophetick Verſe.

Good Days, Good Deeds do ſtill beget.
But the Bad Deeds the bright Angels Let,
Dark Influence, to Dark Acts give Birth,
But here the Stars Light, Joy, and Mirth.

Obſervations on Remarkable Days, to know how the whole Year will ſucceed in weather, Plenty, &c.

IF the *Sun* ſhine clear and bright on *Chriſtmas-day*, it promiſeth a peaceable Year, from *Clamours* and *Strife*, and Fore-tells much plenty to Enſue: But if the *wind* blow *ſtormy*, towards the *Sun-ſet*, it betokens *Sickneſs* in the *Spring*, and *Autumn Quarters*.

If it be *Lowering*, or *wet*, on *Childermas* or *Innocents-day*, it threatens Scarcity, and Mortality among the weaker Sort of young People, but if the Day be very fair it promiſeth plenty.

If *New Year's Day* in the Morning open with *Dusky Red Clouds*, it denotes Strifes and Debates among Great Ones, and many Robberies to happen that Year.

If *January* 25 (being St *Paul's-day*) be Fair, it promiſes a happy Year, but if *Cloudy*, *windy*, or *Rainy*, otherways: hear in this Caſe what an Antient Judicious *Aſtrologer* writes.

If S Paul *be fair and clear,*
It promiſes then a happy Year:
But if it chance to Snow or Rain,
Then will be dear all ſorts of Grain.

Or

Or if the Wind do blow aloft,
Great stirs will vex the World full oft,
And if dark Clouds do muff the Sky,
Then Fowl, and Cattle oft will Die.

It is Remarkable on Shrove-Tuesday, that as the Sun Shine little or much, on that day, or as other Weather happens, so shall every day participate more or less, of such Weather till the end of Lent.

Mists, or Hoar Frosts, on the Tenth of March, betokens a plentiful Year, but not without some Diseases

If the Sun Shines clear on Palm-Sunday, or Easter-day, or either of them, there will be great store of Fair Weather, plenty of Corn, and other Fruits of the Earth

If it Rains on Ascension day, though never so little, it fore-tells a Scarcity to ensue that Year, and Sickness particularly among Cattle; but if it be fair and pleasant, then to the contrary, and pleasant Weather mostly till Michaelmas

If it happens to Rain on Whitsunday, much Thunder and Lightning will follow, Blasts, Mildews &c. But if it be Fair, great plenty of Corn.

If Midsummer-day, be never so little Rainy, the Hazel and Wall-nut will be Scarce: Corn smitten in many Places, but Apples, Pears, and Plumbs, will not be hurt.

If on St. Swithen's-day it proves Fair, a temperate Winter will follow: But if Rainy, Stormy, or Windy, then the contrary

If St Bartholomew's-day be Misty, the Morning beginning with a Hoar Frost, then cold Weather will soon ensue, and a sharp Winter, attended with many biting Frosts.

If *Michaelmas-day* be Fair, the Sun will shine much in the *Winter*, though the Wind at *North East* will frequently Reign long, and be very sharp and nipping.

If in the fall of the *Leaf*, in *October*, many of them Wither on the Bows, and Hang there, it betokens a Frosty *Winter*, with much Snow.

Other Curious Observations on the seasons of the Year; as to the Weather that will happen, and such like Matters.

GReat Observations to predict what will fall out, have been made upon Oak Apples in September: If Cut they have Spiders in them, it betokens Blast, and Infection: If Flys, a dry Season. If Maggots, a great Increase of the Fruits of the Earth: If Spungy and Hollow, without any thing in them, scarcity of the Fruits of the Earth the ensuing Year: If early Ripe, the Winter will soon advance very sharp: If Dry, a dry Winter: If very moist, much Wet, drisling Snow, Rain, and cold moist Winds ensue: If the inner part (between both) fair and clear, then a plentiful Summer will ensue, the Weather Fair and Temperate.

Another Observation is made on the Beech Tree, which Note on this manner: On All-hallows day, cut of some of the Bark, and after that a Chip, or little piece of Wood, cut it, if it be dry, then the ensuing Winter will be dry, but pretty warm and temperate, if moist, a wet Winter.

If on St. Andrew's-day, in the Evening, much Dew or Wet remain on the Grass, it betokens a wet Season to follow, if dry, then the contrary.

If the Nutt Trees Flower much, it betokens great Plenty of Corn that Year: Yet a sickly season in Autumn, and a cold Winter.

Infallible signs of Weather in all Seasons throughout the Year, by the Planets, Elements, Creatures, &c.

SInce many have made Conjectures of Weather, and frequently failed in their Predictions, I have now thought fit, for the advantage of the industrious Husband Man, and others, to lay down unerring Rules and Observations, whereby the various sorts of Weather, with their sudden Changes may be known at all times, not only for one Year, but for Ever, viz. Rain, Wind, excessive Heat or Cold, Snow, Hail, Frost, Thunder and Lightning; sudden Whirl winds and Tempests, &c. And of these in their order.

Infallible signs of Rain, and drisling Weather, taken by Observation of the Planets, and other Stars, Elements, Creatures, &c.

MArk the Sun rising, and if it looks broader than usual, then many moist Vapours are gathering from the Sea, the Air as thickening, and the Sun-beams diffused in it, makes the Face of that Planet show greater than usual, and in a little time you will see the Clouds muster and spread the face of the Heavens, and the Air densing into a watery Body, and if this happen in Hot Weather, viz. Summer or Autumn, violent showers will fall but not of long Continuance: But if in Winter or Spring, settled Rains, but more moderate.

If the Sun Rises with a blewish Circle inclining to white, the Air is gross, and Rain will soon ensue.

The Sun ſetting in a black Cloud, and diffuſing or ſpreading its Beams pailiſh to the North, and South, Prognoſticates a Rainy Night and Morning.

The Sky of a Dusky-red in the Morning, and the Sun riſing pale, an Over-caſting will ſoon enſue, and Rain quickly follow upon it, attended with whisking Winds and Florries.

The often ſhifting of the Wind is a ſign of Rain, eſpecially in Winter and Spring.

Many ſmall Clouds at North Weſt in the Evening ſhows that Rain is gathering, and will ſuddenly fall.

The Moons Horns blunt at its riſing Three Days after the Change, denotes Rainy Weather for that Quarter, but the other Quarters ſeaſonable Weather.

The Stars ſeeming bigger than uſual, pale, dull, and not twinkling, ſhow the Air is thickening to Rain, which will ſoon fall.

Many Stars appearing in the Night, ſeeming a greater Number than uſual, the Wind Eaſt in Summer, fore-ſhows ſudden Rain.

The Signs of Rain by Creatures, &c

WHen the Hern or Bitron, flies low, the Air is Groſs, and thickening into ſhowers.

When Kine view the Sky, ſtretching up their Heads, and ſnuffing the Air, moiſt Vapours are Engendering; and the cauſe of their doing ſo, is their ſenſibleneſs of the Airs ſudden alteration from Dry to Wet, and ſudden Pain will enſue, though at that time the Sun may ſhine out.

The Chattering of Swallows, and their Flying low about Ponds and Lakes, denotes Rain.

The

The Froggs much Croaking in Ditches and Pools, &c. in the Evening foretells Rain in little time to follow. Also the sweating of Stone Pillars, or Tombs, denotes Rain

The Ants Removing their Eggs, denotes Rain, for a secret Instinct in Nature, finding the Air changed in o much Moistness, they carry them to a place of dryer security

The Crows flocking in large Flights, holding their Heads upwards as they fly, and Crying louder than usual, is a sign of Rain as also their stalking by Ponds and Rivers, and sprinkling themselves.

The often Doping and Diving of Water Fowls, fore shows Rain is at Hand.

The Peacocks much Crying, denotes Rain.

Cattle leaving off to Feed, and hasting to shelter under Hedges Bushes. Trees, Out houses, &c. shows sudden showers of Rain are coming

And of this to conclude Rainy Weather, I shall tell you a pleasant, but true Story.

A Gentleman who Travelled much, seeing a Shepherd by the Road side tending his Flocks and other Cattle, demanded of him, if it would continue that Day as it then was, for the Sun shine out. The Shepherd looking on his Cattle, told him, it would Rain very much in an Hour, and extreamly Wet him, unless he got Shelter: The Gentleman smiled at this, and would not believe him, but as he said, so it proved, for immediately a little Cloud Rising at South-West, came driving on with the Wind, and spread it self, so that the Sky was covered with prodigious blackness, and tho' the Gentleman Rid hard to get to a Town about five Miles from him, the Rain e'er he reached it, poured down so prodigiously, that he was

Wet, to the Skin, and remembring what the Shepherd said, that upon his Return finding him in the same place, he Requested he would tell him how he came so precisely to know the Change of the Weather; the Shepherd at first refused it, but for half a Crown (after much Importunity) consented, and when the Gentleman expected he should express himself in Astrological Terms, he only said, Sir, do you see yonder Py'd Colt, pointing to him Well, said the Gentleman, and what of that? Why, says the Shepherd, when he runs his Head into the Hedge, and turns his Arse to the Weather gage, then it will certainly Rain, tho' the Weather promises at that time otherways to those that are Ignorant of Skill in Prognosticating: This may be (says the Gentleman) but that will it signifie to me on my Journey, seeing I can't carry such an Almanack as your Colt in my Pocket; however the Gentleman was highly pleased, and concluded his Money well laid out But here I have Out-done the Shepherd, in giving so many Prognosticks, that be where you will, you cannot miss of some of them to inform you.

Signs of Wind, and sudden Storms arising Prognosticated by the Planets, Elemente, Creatures, &c. in all seasons of the Year for ever.

IF the Moon blushes, and is Redder than usual, Winds are engendered, and storms will arise.

If at Sun-rising pale spots seem to appear in its Orb, and dazle there, strong Winds will ensue from the South, the Wind soon shifting thither in what ever Quarter before it was.

Meteors, or as some calls them Stars shooting swiftly, and spreading a long Train of Light, fore-run Winds that will soon ensue. Chaff

Chaff, Leaves, Feathers, Thiſtle Down, or ſuch light Things whisking about, and turning round, fore-ſhews Tempeſtuous Winds.

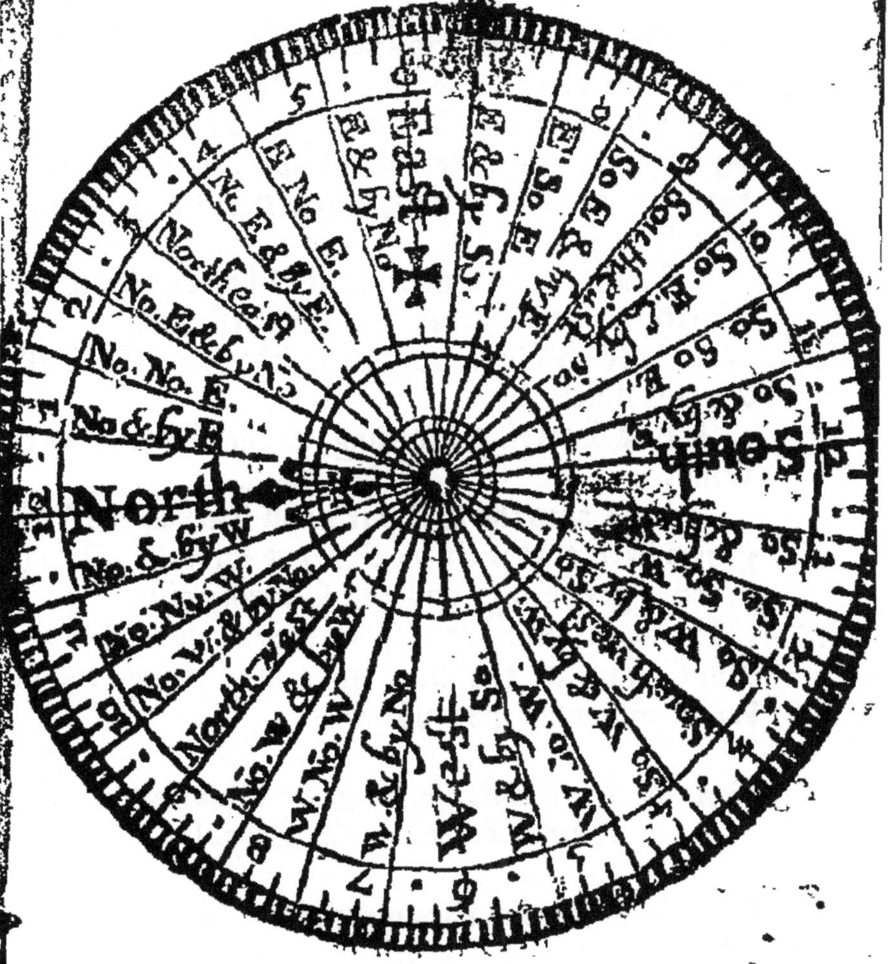

A murmering noiſe in the Woods, when little Wind is ſtirring, fortells a Storm is Engendring.

Cormorants, and other Sea Fowl flocking to ſhore, and often Crying, denotes great ſtorms to enſue.

Cattle on a ſudden haſting to their Stalls, Houſing places, or other Shelter, do the like

The Hern exceeding high flying, denotes the Air is moved with Winds, in the Upper Region, and that ſudden ſtorms will enſue.

The much Whiſpering, and Ruſling among Reeds and Flaggs, in Meadows, Ditches, and Marſhes, Prognoſticates the Wind is gathering in the Air.

Small ſcattering Clouds to the South Weſt, that fly high, lye as it were in Ridges, and ſeem not to move, engender Winds, often producing Whirl-Winds.

A kind of a Murmering of Thunder from the North, fore-tells great Tempeſts will ariſe.

A Reddiſh Circle about the Moon at the Full, denotes much Wind.

A Red Lowring Morning, is the Forerunner of Wind.

If in a Lamp the Oyl purls and ſparkle, the Wick grows hard, that it Burns dimly it foretells a ſtrong Wind engendering, and will ſuddenly riſe.

If their appear Fiery ſpots; or thoſe of a Reddiſh Colour in the Sun upon its Setting, much Wind will enſue ſpeedily.

Signs of the Winds ſhifting or Changing in the ſeveral Points of the Compaſs.

WHen the Sun riſes with many pale ſpots, appearing in its Orb, and part of it Vailed in a Cloud, the Wind in what Point ſoever, it will ſoon ſhift to the South.

When the Wind has been ſettled 24 Hours or more, in any of the Full Points, as North-East, West

West, and South, when it begins to shift, it will not settle till it comes to the oppesite Point, as from the North to the South, and so from the Full East, to Full West, and so of the Angular Points, as for the North East, to South East.

Let the Wind be in what Quarter it will, upon the New Moon it presently shifts.

When the Generality of the Clouds Rack, or Drive with the Wind, yet may in little Fleeces or long strakes, lying higher, and appear not to move the Wind is Flagging, and will quickly shift.

Signs of Storms Ceasing.

A Hasty shower of Rain falling when the Wind has Raged for some Hours, soon allays it.

If a Storm rise with the Sun, at the Falling of the Sun it will begin to Decline, and about Mid-Night Cease.

If the Water Ruckles much, and frequent Bubles arise the Storm is of a short continuance

If a Halcyons or King Fishers, and a Bird so called, attempts the Seas when the Wind blows hard, it is a sign it is Abating, and will soon cease.

The uneasiness of Swine in their Stys, and their endeavouring to be enlarged, denotes the Wind in a little time to cease

The Merry Chiriping of Sparrows, does the like, as also the Moles coming out of their Holes.

Signs of Excessive Hot Weather.

Little strings like Cobwebs; flying in the Air in a Morning show the Heat will be much, especially for the Season.

A Gliſſening on the Graſs at the Sun Riſe, like the Thread of Spinners, denotes much Heat in Summer, or Autumn.

The ſteeming and ſmoaking of ſtanding Water, when the Sun is about ſetting, fortells a Hot Day to enſue; for then the Mineral Firs are forcing their way to add to the Sun's Enflaming the Air.

Great ſwarms of Gnatts abroad in Marſhes and Fenny Places in the Evening, fore-tells Hot Weather to enſue.

Many Frogs coming out of the Water on the Banks of Ditches, Ponds, &c. preſage Hot Weather to enſue.

The Plover or Lapwing Flying high, and then low, making almoſt continual Crys, fore ſhews much Heat to follow.

Signs of Cold Weather, or hard Winter.

THE Sun's ſetting in the Miſt, looking Red, and Broader than uſual.

The Clearneſs of the Stars, and their much Twinkling.

Starlings Feldeſares, and other Birds of a Hot Nature, haſtening in great Flocks and Flights from the Northern to the Southern Climate.

Cold Dews, and Morning Rhymes on St. Bartholomew's Day, and the three ſucceeding Days.

A Hoar Froſt on Michaelmas Day in the Morning, denotes a hard Winter.

The Swallows going away ſooner than uſual, denotes a Cold Seaſon to enſue.

The Birds laying up Haws, Slows, and other Stores in old Neſts, or Holiows of Trees, foretells a hard Winter.

Sea

Sea-Pyes Flocking from Salt Water about Fresh Rivers or Lakes, signifies a sudden alteration of the Weather to much Cold.

The Owl much Hooting in the Night, at Michaelmas Tide, denotes a hard frosty Winter.

Ignis Fatuus, or Will with a Whisp; much and often appearing in Moorish Ground, fore-runs a Cold Season.

Prognosticks of Fair Weather by the Planets, Elements, and Creatures, &c.

THE Moon at four Days Old having her Horns sharp and pointed very Bright, it predicts fair Weather till the Full, if not to the Month's End.

The Stars shine Clear and Bright, seeming to Dart or Shoot out pointed Rays.

Little Clouds sinking Low, as into Valleys at South East, and South West

The Sun rising in the Morning Fair and Bright, and setting at Night Blushing, without Spots or Black Clouds near it.

The Larks rising very high, and continuing singing a long time.

The Halcyons, and other Sea Fowl leaving the Shores and Flocking to Sea.

Mists or smoakings on the top of the Water.

The Rainbow appearing after a shower; and the Blew and Yellow part of it very Bright and Lightish Colour.

Fish often Rising and Bubling at the top of the Water, Cattle Feeding without often looking upon or about them.

Scattering white Clouds, like Fleeces of Wool to the North West.

Spiders

Spiders Webs on the Grass and Trees, fore-tells much fair Weather.

Bees flying far from their Hives, and coming late Home, do the like.

A Bright, Clear, or Shining Circle about the Moon at the Full, promises fair Weather, predicts many fair Days to ensue

Much Dew on Sheeps Wool in a Morning, is a sign of fair Weather.

Signs of Hail (violent and Moderate) by the Planets, Elements, &c.

IF the Sun at Rising cast a Glittering Light, as if it Reflected on some Lucid Matter, tho' few or no Clouds at that time appear, the Vapours are Condensed in the Cold Region, and fore running into Clouds, that will scatter Violent Hail.

If (in the Morning) the Estearn Skys before the Suns Rising look pale, and Refracted Beams appear in Thick Clouds, great storms of Hail will ensue, to the great Damage of Corn, Vine-yards, Fruits, Trees, *&c.*

If the Clouds looks Fleecy Duskey white enclining to Yellowish, and move but Heavily, though the Wind is pretty stiff, the Vapours Composing them, are Engendered and Frozen, as *Virgil* says.

Ah then, but I'll defend her Grapes,
Such horr'd Hail on House tops Ratling Leaps.

If the Clouds appear of a whitish blue, and Expend much, it will be small Hail or Drisling; for that happens in Winter, or the Spring when it cannot be carried high enough to be Condensed with a greater quantity of Cold, because the Re-

fracted

fracted Sun beams are weak in their *Operation*, and this appears by a *Curling* or *Curdling* in the *Clouds* as they *Rise*, and appearance *Expand* themselves.

Signs of Snow, and Drisly sleet, &c.

CLouds like Woolly Fleeces appearing high, and moving heavily, the middle a darkish pale, and edges white, carry Snow in them, that in the *Winter* Frozen in Sheets, by Cold *East*, *North East*, or *North West* Winds, pressing hard on the *Air* (no longer able to bear them up) shiver in the Fall, and break into Flakes, resembling many Figures, as *Stars*, *Leaves of Trees*, *Flowers*, &c. If he *Clouds* be pressed nearer the *Earth*, the *Vapours* so Frozen is Grosser, and the Flaked are Larger, but more Remorse, thinner and so fall in a Sleet, or little Flakes

The Sun's looking pale at Rising the much Lowring of *Cattle* in the Field The Croaking of *Ravens*, and *Birds* fliging their Wings, fore-show it.

Drisle is a kind of a *Ryme* or Mists; Ascending and Freezing, and to be foreseen as the foregoing.

Prognosticks of Frosty Weather by the Planets, Elements, Creatures &c.

THE *Stars* looking bright and twinkling much, shows a *Cold Air*, *Engendering* Frosts.

The *Sky* seeming fuller of *Stars* than usual, and the *Wind* suddenly shifting to the *East*, or *North-East*, after the Change of the *Moon*, in the Winter, denotes a setting *Frost* of long Continuance.

The *Owls Hooping* often with a louder Note than usual, denotes a *Frost* at hand. The

The *Sun's setting* Red in a *Mist*, and a White Fogg creeping low in a Marshy or Moorish Ground, shows the Air Condensing into *Cold*.

The Sea-cole Fire Burning *Blue* (that is) a great part of the Flame, and scorching more than usual, fore-tells a *Frost* at hand, or if it begun, its continuance.

The *Moon* shewing bright, with sharp *Horns* after the Change, denotes the Air is Raresying, and *Cold Weather* will soon set in to freeze the *Earth*.

A *Hoary Ryme* sticking on *Trees*, *Bushes*, and *Pales*, in the Morning, foretells sharp bleak *Winds* will soon set in, and contract a bitter *Frost*.

Little *Clouds* hovering low in the *North*, when none any where else appear, fore runs *Cold freezing Winds and Snow*.

Signs of a great Thaw in any hard Frost, &c.

THE Sun's looking waterish at its Rising, is a sign the Frost will break

The *Wind* having held long and extream sharp in one *Point*, suddenly shifting, brings a Relenting, if not a thorow *Thaw*

The Sun's setting in *Blueish Clouds*, and casting *Refracted Beams* into them, bids the *Frost* prepare to be gone.

The *Stars* looking dull, and the *Moon's Horns* blunted, fore-tell a Change in *Nature*.

Of wonderful Signs in the Heavens, and on the Earth, whence they Proceed, and what they Prognosticate of strange Events

I Now come to treat of *Meteors*, and strange Sights, and Impressions in the *Air*, and on the

the *Earth*, *Prognosticating* many Wonderful, and Amazing Things to ensue: so far I conceive Proper to the Subject in Hand.

Comets, Blazing Stars; with Astrological Observations, what they are, and Prognosticks on them.

A *Comet* or *Blazing Star* is formed of an Exhalation, hot and dry, being a great quantity of Unctious *Vapours*, drawn up in the highest *Region*, and they meet with approaching the *Region*

gion of *Fire*, are Kindled, appearing when the *Sun Beams* are of it, like a real *star*, with a *Blazing Tail*, though it be many Thousand Miles beneath the *Fiery Region*, and sometimes it moves after the motion of the *Air*, which is Circular, but it never goeth down out of the Compass of Sight, and so continue till the matter that feeds them is Consumed, and then Expire; the time of their Generation is oftenest in Harvest, or Autumn, for in the Spring their is too much Moisture, and too little Heat to Generate them In Summer their is too much Heat, that will Disperse and Consume the matter, that it cannot be Joyned together, and in Winter, the Cold and Moisture contrary to the Nature of a Comet opposes it.

These fore-run many Calamities, and the Reason is this:

1*st*. Great Droughts ensue, because the Comet cannot be Generated without great Heat, and much Moisture is Consumed in the Burning of it.

2*d*. Barrenness of the Earth, because the fitness of the Earth is drawn up, whereof the Comet chiefly consists; so that the Earth wanting that Oily Substance, grows Steril, and produces not as at other times.

3*d*. Pestilence, for as much as this kind of Exhalation in long Burning, Expiring or going out, Diffuseth itself, and Currupteth the Air with a Poisonous Infection, and that drawn in by us as our common Breath, Infecteth the Bodies of Men with Plagues, Violent Fevers, or other Excessive Hot Diseases, and the like Effects they consequently have on the Bodies of Beasts, that suck in the same Airs, working on them by

Mur-

Murrens, Swellings, Breakings out of Boils, Blains, and the like, proceeding from poisonous Infection

The Learned have noted, that after the appearing of Commets, other great Calamities befal, as Wars, Seditions, Changes in State, the Death of Princes and Noblemen And thus *Virgil:*

As in moist Night a Blazing Comet *streams,*
With Bloody Omens Red, and Syrius *Beams,*
Brings to sad Mortals, Sicknesses and Thirsts,
And Heaven in Mourning hangs, with Influence Curst.

For (say they) at what time the Comets do shine, there be many Hot and Dry Exhalations in the Air, which Influence the Natural Temper of the Hot, Dry, and Cholerick Persons, whereby they are quickly stirred to Anger, to raise Wars, Tumults, or Contentions. Also those nice Bodies, living at Ease, are of a soft delicious Temper So the Infection seizes them sooner than Labourious hard faring Bodies, for in Plagues it hath been observed, that the most delicate Fed and Tender Bodies, are soonest Infected and swept away. I might enlarge on this, but my proposed Brevity constrains me to Desist and proceed to other Matters

Many Suns appearing in the Heavens at once, the Cause, and what they predict.

OFten to the Appearance of Men, two, or many times three Suns have appeared in the Firmament at once; tho' in reality but one real Sun, the other being the Images or Impressions of it, in condensed Air, or watery Clouds, for they are nothing

thing but the Idols, or Images of the real Sun, that daily enlightens the World, represented by its Beams, impressing in an equally thick and smooth gross Air, or Cloud, placed on the side of the Sun, and sometimes on both sides, into which the Sun-beams being Received, as into a Glass, expresseth the likeness and fashion of Light, which is in the Sun so appearing to us, who are a vast distance beneath it, as if there were many Suns.

This thick and watery Air or Clouds, is not directly under the Sun, for when it is, it makes the Circle about it called the Crowns or Garlands, or if it were opposite to the Sun, it will form the Rainbow, of which I shall speak hereafter, but on the sides where the Images may be best Reflected and Represented

These are often seen in the Morning and Evening, about the Rising and going down of the Sun, though sometimes at other Hours, and sometimes there appear many little Suns, like unto Stars, which are caused by many little divided Clouds, as the Reflection of a Man's Face appears in all parts of a broken Glass: Or as a Multiplying Glass makes one thing seem many.

The appearing of these Phenomenas, naturally betoken Tempests, and much Rain to ensue: Because they cannot appear but in watery Disposition of the Air.

Also if they appear on the South side of the Sun, they signify more violent Showers than on the *North*, and the reason is the hot Southern Vapour is sooner dissolved into Water, then the colder *Northern* ones.

As for a supernatural Signification, they have been noted to have portened the Condition of Prin-

Princes for Kingdoms, as not long before the Contention of *Gelba*, *Otha*, and *Vitellius* for the Empire of *Rome*, three Suns appeared: Also, a little before the Slaughter of *Lewes*, King of *Hungary*, in a Battle against the *Turks*, were seen three Suns, denotes the three Princes that afterward Contended for the Kingdoms, *viz Ferdinand* King of *Bohemia*, *John Wayvode*, of *Transilvania*, and *Solomon* Emperor of the *Turks*.

The appearing of many Moons in the Night, and what they Prognostick of Good or Bad

AS for the cause of many Moons, appearing or seeming to do so at once, I need not repeat it again, but only tell you the cause is the same as that of the Sun; **Pikney** calls these Night Suns, because they joyn with the Light of the Moon, and Augment its Light in wonderful measure, whilst they continue.

They foretell great Rains, and wet Season to follow, producing Land Floods, and doing much Harm to Corn and Grass, if grown up; also the Overflowing of Rivers, and the Breaking in of the Sea; and in general a moist wet Year (or part of a Year as they fall Earlier or Later) to ensue to the End, which will occasion scarcity of Corn, and other Fruits of the Earth.

Of the Rainbow (how caused) and what it Prognosticates

HAving promised to say something more particularly of the Rainbow, which gives a great insight to the Weather, immediately to follow: I shall treat of it here, as it most probably follows in Order.

The

The Rainbow is the Apparition of certain Colours, in a Cloud opposite against the Sun, in a half Circle as *Virgil* seems to hint, when he makes *Iris* or the Rainbow Messengers to *Juno*, viz.

From Heaven then Dew rose wing'd Iris flew,
She 'gainst the Sun a Thousand Colours drew,
Plac'd on her Head, &c.

The Sun reflecting on a Cloud at a distance from it sideways, and Refracting its Beams there lively by its Light, shews the various Colours the Clouds is Composed of, *Posidonious* Terms the Rainbow the Sun's Looking glass, wherein its Image is Represented, and that the blue Colour is the proper Colour of the Air or Cloud, and the red of the Sun, that the other are mixed Colours, or Colours of Conixtion. And indeed the Colours more admirably lively than can be represented any where else. But since Rainbows are so often Visible, I think I may spare the Labour of a particular Description of them Therefore I proceed to what they Prognosticate in Relation to Weather, *viz*

From that part first the Rainbow first begins to break, or vanish, Winds will arise, and bring great showers.

If the Rainbow vanishes as it were altogether, fair Weather will ensue.

If it be broken in many parts, tempestuous Winds are gathering in the Air.

If (after it appear) the Colours wax grosser and darken, Rain is gathering, if light, and the Colours fairer, the contrary, and guess of other Aspects in the Rainbow.

Of

Of the Ignis Fatuus, *or Fires that lead People astray in the Night time, called the* Will with the Whisp.

THese in *Popish*, superstitious Times were held to be the Souls that had escaped out of Purgatory, to desire the Prayers of the living, upon the Earth, for their admission to Paradise, because they were often seen in Church Yards, where Unctious Vapours arise from the steem of dead Bodies, since they are called *Will with the Whisp*, or as the *Latins* calls them, *Ignis Fatuus*; *foolish Fire*, because they are rather a fire in shew, then a real one in truth.

It is a Fire, or Resemblance of it, that seemeth to go before Men, or follow them in the Night, and lead them out of their Way into Waters, or other dangerous Places, it is a weak exhalation kindled by reason of a violent motion in a Cold Night, in the lowest Region of the Air. For in the hot Season they appear not. It is imbodied by the Cold, and shut in as it were in a Bladder, and its motion is from that of the Air; For that being as it were of a piece, tho' innumerable particles, is agitated with violent motions, and as the body of a Man moves in breaking it, the whole sensibly suffer, which makes this Nocturnal Light move swiftly, and press towards the Party moving, it dancing and playing about him. So that the affright, and that many times, by that Means in a dark Night, makes him wonder, and being once out, he knows not how to get into the right way again, and often Mischief ensue, by his tumbling into one bad place or another.

When these Exhalations rise much, which they mostly do in moorish or foggy Grounds. In Autumn,

tumn, and the beginning of Winter, they fore-run a cold sharp Winter, but a *fruitful Summer* to ensue, because it shews the cold Vapours will not rise high, but remain nearer the Earth, and oppress it with still Frosts, more than blustering Winds: and again, in so doing the Earth in Winter will spend little of its Heat, or Evaporate its Unctious Quality to any great Degree, which working with its nitrous part, is the cause of Fertility, and causes encrease of all kind of Vegetives, to a very great degree more than ordinary.

Of the Flame that appears on the Hair and Beards of Men, and upon that of Beasts.

THis by some has been taken to be wonderfully strange, and of such Terror, that some have been extreamly affrighted by it, supposing it was the Devil come to involve them in sulpherous flames, when the cause is really natural. For these Fires are sometimes clammy Exhalations scattered abroad in the Air in small parts, which in the Night, by the Resistance of the Cold, agitating in a violent Motion, are kindled and rushing on where they find Opposition, by reason of their clammy Nature, stick, and appear a blue Fire, very affrighting to those at a Distance; when the Persons on whom they fasten, perhaps perceive them not, or at least not presently.

When they are much abroad, they fore-tell high Winds, and blustering stormy Winds, a wet Spring, and a dry Summer, very sickly, but fruitful.

Strange

Strange Apparitions of Armies, and other wonderful Sights in the Air, how caused.

APparitions in the Air, are only Exhalations in the lowest or highest Region of it, not really Fires, but seem so by the Sun or Moon reflecting Light on them.

The Light in this case is instead of white, and the dark shaddow sets off the Figures; such Apparitions seem terribly to represent, and (diversly mixed according to the divers Dispositions of the Exhalation, they cause variety of Colours, according to the thickness or thinness of the Exhalation, presenting to the Imagination of fond fancisul Mortals) Armies in Battle, Seas, and Navie engaging on them, spacious Fields, Houses, Castles, and the like, though indeed but Airy Phantoms. However they fore-run Storms, and are accompanied with Flashes of Lightning very often, and in the hotter Weather, with prodigious Claps of Thunder, if the Clouds are gross, and full of Water, looking a greenish dark in the middle, tho' about the Edges, the Light may as in the thinner parts, point various Colours, being composed of hot and *moist Exhalations*; and though these are looked on as supernatural Causes, they are no more than the effect of Nature.

The Kinds of Earthquakes, their Cause, and Signs, fore running them, and what they portend.

IN this Treatise I cannot but make some Observation on the Cause of Earthquakes, considering of late Years, we have been so much alarumed

larumed with their prodigious Effect, and so few people knew what natural Effect produces them, for wonderful Things are related by Historians concerning them, but the best Opinions given of their causes, and the probable, is, That extraordinary qualities of heat and Cold, shut up in the vast Caverns of the Earth, contending for Mastey, and pressing violently to go out, but find Opposition by the too much dryness or moisture of the Porus parts of the Earth, seek a way to vent themselves by force, and break their way through all Opposition.

The Signs of an Earth Quake being at hand, is, the much rising of the Sea, or other great Waters, when no visible cause is seen to occasion it, for then the Vapours labouring to force their way to open Air, first finding a more easy Passage there, than on the firm Land, first make their way, and boil up the Weathers, as it were to force through them

Also a cold Calmness of the Air is another Sign, for then the Exhalation that should be abroad, is forcibly pent up in the Earth, and struggling to get out with violence.

Others Observe, that whether the Sky is as it were Clear, some long strakes of Clouds are however seen, but the most certain, is a rumbling murmuring Noise in the Earth, and as kind of whistleing Wind whisking about the Air, being troubled, for then the fore-runner, or thinest part of the Vapour is spiring out, to make way for the greater Shock, and more violent gross shock of it, yet however, the Cause is the same, notwithstanding the manner of shaking the Earth is different, as I shall briefly Note.

The

The First is when the Earth is shaken Laterally or to one side, which is when the whole force of the enclosed Vapout driveth to one side or place, and there is no contrary Motion to let it, if the Vapour be weak, it only makes a Rocking or Trembling; but if violent, breaks out, overthrowing the mightiest Buildings from their Foundations, and by such an Earthquake (in the Reign of *Tiberius* the *Roman* Emperor) twelve great Cities in *Asia* were levelled in one, and most of their Inhabitants buried in the Ruins, and sad have those been of late at *Naples* in *Italy*; also in the Island of *Sicily*, and *Lima*, and *Jamaica* in the *West-Indies*. I will not mention what happened in *England* lately; which was rather a Trepidation, than an Earthquake Yet it caused much Consternation, and the excessive quantity of Vapours, that then effused, in all probility, have occasioned the Climate to be the Colder to this Day.

A Second kind of Earthquake lifts up the Earth, so that falling on a sudden, and lets it fall again: This happens when the Wind in a great Mass strugles on a sudden to Evaporate · But the Opposition is too strong, and forces it down again

The third is that which breaks its way violently through, causing openings, gaupings of the Earth, So that Towers, Cities, Mountains, and hugh standing Waters have been swallowed up and lost: All these are very Terrible, and are in the hot Season, accompanied with prodigious Thunders and Lightnings And the Vapours' pressing too much infection upon the Air, before it can be refined and purged, it infects the Bodies of Men and Beasts, causing mortal Diseases: And the Earth having spent so much, that it cannot in a plentiful manner assist to produce fertility, a scarcity ensues not only for the present, but for some Years after, till the Recruit comes to make the Ground more fertil, &c.

Signs fore-running Thunder, Lightning, &c.

METeors shooting in the Night in Summer-time, denotes the Air inflamed with much Heat, and that Thunder and Lightning will ensue.

Many Clops and Clefts in the Ground, signify that the fiery Vapours are ascended from the Earth, and have so Dried and Parched it in their Passage: So that the fire being mounted so soon as thick Clouds Over-cast the Sky, the grosser part of the Fire descending, and struggling with the watery Clouds to get a passage through, is that which is called the Lightning.

If no Clouds appear in sultry Weather, and the Sun sets Red and Fiery, great Flashes will appear in the North, and North West, which is called Fulgetrum, and is Lightning. But not meeting with Opposition, it carries no Thunder with it, though springing from the same Cause, but wanting Opposition, the Noise is not heard.

Of sudden Whirl-winds, and surprizing Tempests.

WHirl-winds, or Vapours suddenly Rising out of the Earth, and gathering in the Air, imbodied in Clouds, and stretching them break forth Violently. So forcing the way to the Earth, with much Fury in a Narrow Compass, as it were inclosed, they Circle round, and Hurry ry things about Violently, often Over-turning Houses, Barns, Sheep-Cots and Lifting People, and Cattle into the Air, letting them Fall again many times to their Destruction, though in these Countries they are not so violent, as others nearer the Line, where Vapours are carried up more violently by the Heat.

The Signs that fore-run them, is a troubled Sky, the Whisking and Circling Light Things about, when as yet there appears little or no Wind, a Murmuring heard in the Air, the Air beating down right, as it were upon the Water, and making it Wrinkle: Trees Whisking in one place, and not in another.

Approved Rules for Managing Husbandry, or Rural Affairs, during the Twelve Months of the Year for ever.

In JANUARY.

LAY Warm Dung to the Roots of your young Choice Trees and Plants · Lop and take off Superfluous Branches in the New Moon: If the Weather be Open set Beans, sow Pease, Parsnip Seeds, dig and trench your Ground, especially in Gardens, give your Cattle gentle Drenches: and to the more Sickly, and Weak, warm Marshes of Bran and Malt sodden in Water, keep them warm Housed, if the Weather be extream Cold, and Cover your Choice Plants and Flowers.

In FEBRUARY.

Cut Quicklets, and supply the Decayed Places with New Ones, Plant Vines, Hops, Liquorish, and all Shrubs bearing Fruit, sow Onions, Pease,

Beans, Salleting, for the Spring, and Pot-Herbs, Moss Fruit Trees, and Prune them, take off Superfluous Branches, not yet Removed, Graft on Young Stocks, and Manure Barren Soile with Dung, and other Manure, to *Render it Fertile*, lay Traps for *Vermine*.

In MARCH.

The Weather being open, and the Wind not in the Cold Quarters, Cover the Roots of Fruit Trees that before were Open with Dung, Set Quicksets, and Graft choice Siens, sow Barley, Oats, Onions, Parsnips, Carrots, Mellions; Set Artichoaks, Sage, and all kind of Pot-Herbs; Bleed and Geld Cattle in the Wane of the Moon; Sow all manner of Garden Seeds for the Spring and Summer store.

In APRIL.

Sow Flax, Hemp, and Pole your Hops, set and sow what Plants and Herbs were before wanting, open the Mouths of your Bee-hives, clean their stools, and rub them over with sweet Herbs to Cherish, Cheer, and Enable them to take the more Pleasure in their Labour, upon their first coming out, weed Gardens and Corn, prepare for Dary-Work, Bark Trees, and Raise Choice Flowers.

In MAY.

In the beginning of this Month, sow and set all manner of tender SummerHerbs, continue to weed, trim up your Hop Gardens, cut off Superfluous Branches, weed Corn, Distil Cordial Waters, make Conserves, drive Rivers, and drain Plashes.

In

In JUNE.

Shear your Sheep the Moon Encreasing, Geld your Lambs and Calves, the Moon decreasing, sow Lettice, and Redishes, three or four Days after the Full Moon, gather such Herbs as you would keep Dry for the Winter Use, in the Full of the Moon, when the Sun has drawn up the Dew and Moisture from them, set Rosemary and *July*-flowers, and stake up weak Plants and Flowers.

In JULY.

Gather forward Summer Seeds, when the Sun has dryed them, cut off needless Suckers, drive Bees, Mow, Inoculate, Inarch, in the Full Moon, gather the Seeds of such Flowers as are Ripe, dry them in the Sun, then hang them in the Pods to Harden To kill Flees and Bugs, strow Powder of Rue, Worm wood, and Nut-galls, under your Bed.

In AUGUST.

Take the Opportunity of the fairest Weather to Reap in, from the before-mentioned Directions relating to Weather, neither Reap nor Mow Corn too early, let the Sun be pretty well Risen when you begin, and it will prevent much the danger of Musling and Sweatning, gather Garden Seeds within a Day or two of the Moon's Full, lay Traps for Vermine; gather Fruit in Dry Days; sow Seeds for Winter, Salleting and Pot-Herbs.

In SEPTEMBER.

Gather Hops, the Weather being dry, and the Dew off from them, take Honey, make Verjuice, move and set slips of Flowers, remove Young Trees and Plants, making them, but in the Transplantation, they may stand to the same quarter of the Wind they first grew; do this in the New of the Moon, the Wind at *South* or *west* · cut Quicksets, and gather Winter Fruits without Bruising: sow Wheat and Rye; sow Parsnips, Carrots, and Turnips for Winter store.

In OCTOBER.

Continue to sow Wheat and Rye, remove young Trees and Plants in the New of the Moon, cut Rose Trees, Cyprus, Juniper, and Box, set Kernel Stones and Nuts, gather Grapes in the beginning of the Month. The Weather being dry, make an end of gathering Winter Fruit, lay Open the Roots of Fruit Trees, and Trench your Ground: Kill Swine for your Winter store.

In NOVEMBER.

Fell Timber, Moss Fruit Trees, Geld Calves, Purge your Cattle to prevent Diseases Set Crabsticks to Graft on, In the last Quarter of the Moon set Pease and Beans, sow Parsnips and Carrot-Seeds. Trench Garden Ground with Dung, make Drains to carry the Water off.

In DECEMBER.

Continue to fell Timber, set Traps, Sprunges for Hares, Rabbits, and Wild Fowl; cover your choice Flowers, and Plants with Mats or Straw, coat or double cover your Bee hives, Bleed Horses if the Weather be open, and Drench your other Cattle, keep good Fires, Hospitality, and Wholsome warm Dyet, and thus much in general Observations what is to be done relating to Husbandry throughout the Year, which cannot but be of Use to the Honest Country Man, &c.

Signs of Murrein Rot, or such like Destroying Diseases in Cattle, how to Prevent or Remedy them.

CAttle are one main support of the Nation, affording so many Commodities to Man, so, that without their doing well, and Multiplying, we should be but in a bad Condition, therefore it ought to be the Care of those who are most Concerned with them, and to whose particular Advantage they more immediately Redound, to look Carefully to them, and secure their Health as many be. And because Murriens among larger Cattle, and Rots among the Smaller, are the most Fatal of Diseases, and sweep them away by Herds and Flocks, I shall (from long Experience) show the nearest way to fore-see the approaching Danger, which coming for want of such Precaution, or Fore-sight, has Ruined many, and having fore-shewed it, tell how it may be Helped, if in spight of Care it takes Effect. Which sometimes it will do

Signs of Murrein that do befal Cattle.

IF the Moon change 3 Days before St *Bartholomew's* Day it will be a sickly Year amongst Cattle: But this is not the Rule I intend to direct you by, for the observance of the particular, above mentioned; but after that Day is over, and no Rain fallen in the Night, go as soon as it is Day into the Fields of Pasture, where your Cattle are to be kept, and lying down with your Eye against the Sun's rising, as even as you can with the surface of the Earth, and if you perceive a glistering, like Spiders threads, or a white jelly froth or foam on the Grass, then Infectious Vapours are beginning to Rise out of the Earth, and to fall down in poisonous Dews, threatning Infection to the larger sort of Cattle especially: Therefore (for a while) feed them on the higher and drier grounds But if no such thing at this time can be discerned, by reason the weather may be hot, and draw up that Jelly, or whiteness of corrupted Dew, look immediately at the time ordered on *Michaelmas Day* in the Morning: And if you observe it, then it will have the like effects, though somewhat weaker, and the Air less Corrupted To prevent therefore this Murrein, Long-sought: Or as some call it, Gurget: If you are constrained to Pasture your Beasts, bleed them as soon as ever the Leaf begins to fall, peg their Ears and Dew-laps with Hele-bore, or Bears-foot, a Plant so called, drench them with Savin and Rue, boiled in strong Ale, and give them a scowering, and this will prepare them to resist the pestilential Air, and mainly contribute to the preserving them.

If you find however that any of your Beasts (af-
ter afore-named Caution) be swelled under the
Jaws, against the Throat-boul; then draw forth
its Tongue, and open a Vein that lyeth under it,
an Inch a half long-way, and there will corrupt
Blood, and infectious Water issue out: then having
burn Bay-salt and allum, mix them with Vine-
gar, and rub it well into the Wound; this done,
slit the Hide where the swelling outwardly appears
and draw the Skin, so that you make a hollowness
between that and the swelled Flesh, beat together
Spear-grass, burnt Salt and Butter, put this kind
of Poultis into the hollow, between the Skin and
the Flesh, and stitch it together, but not so close
but the infectious Matter may evacuate.

This done, take a Lump of the bluest Clay you
can get, about four pound Weight, boyl it in two
Quarts or more of Man's stale Urine, so much as
(the whole being stirred, after well boyling) will
become thick, bruise a good Handful of the under
bark of young Elder, add this with a handful of salt,
and a quarter of a pound of a rusty Bacon well ma-
shed and beaten to Pieces, stir them continually till
the Ingredients be as thick as pap; then bathe the
Beast's Face faom the Ears downwards, towards
the slit, as hot as he may endure it: so do three
times a day, till the swelling is abated seperating the
infected from the sound Cattle, for fear of its sprea-
ding among them, more than otherwise it would:
Then with an Oyntment made of Butter, Tarr,
and Bees-wax, Anoint the Sore Place as hot as may
be, and in so ordering the Beast will recover,
unless exceeeding far gone before taken in hand.

The like Measures may be taken with Swine, for
the violent swelling in their Throat and Jaws, con-

tracted by an Infection through foul feeding, and bad Airs, discerned by the like symptoms.

Prognosticks of a Rot which fall upon Sheep.

IF it has been a hot close Summer, great heat drops often falling, and little Thunder then on St *Luke*'s Day, which is the 18*th.* of *October*; make the Observations as before directed in the Morning, if the Sun rise clear, otherwise do it as well as you can, and taste the Dews upon the Grass if they be bitter or brackish, the sign is apparent, that it is likely to be unhealthly Year for Sheep, and a fore-runner of the Rot among them, if great precaution be not had to prevent it, especially if they be suffered to feed among old Grass that has not been Mowed, in moist, wet low Grounds, for then taking in a great deal of Water, it makes their Skins loose, and their Lungs full of a Flegmatick water that Rots them Consider then in the first place how they ought to be feed to preserve them, which are so necessary in many Circumstances to us

The Grass good and Wholsome for Sheep, is that among which grows a good quantity of *Melilot*, *Claver*, *Self-heal*, *Cinquefoil*, *Broom*, *Pimpernel*, and *white Henbane*; Also *Sparrow wort*, *Knet-grass*, *Penny wort*, and *Middleweed grass*. For here the Soil promises, not only wholsome Grass: but these are Medicinal, to preserve them against the Infection, that not only causes the Rot, but many other Diseases.

High Grounds, dry and fruitful, are the best Pasture for them, the Grass there being usually short and sweet, but if you cannot avoid putting them in low Grounds for want of other conveniency, take

take care not to bring them from the Fold, till the Sun be risen, and then with your Dog, or otherways chuse them about, till they are well heated, and then let them feed or rest.

This Chasing is many ways advantageous; first, it beats the Mildews from the Grass, and other Dews very hurtful to them in their feeding; likewise kettles, webs, and stakes, which the Sheep licking up in feeding, Contribute to the Rot; it also stirs the Humours in them that wasts the Moisture, and prevents the Effects of Rottenness. They feed also more deliberately, and not so greedily as otherways they would do, chusing their Food, which is most Healthful and Proper.

Once a Month, and oftener in the Raw wet Season, Rub their Mouths with Bay-salt and Vinegar, which in a great Measure is a preservative against Sickness. And thus much to the Ordering them in general For now I come nearer to particulars.

Rot in Sheep, how to prevent it, and other Diseases, and Cure it when taken.

AS to the Rot; particular to Sheep that are for Grazing, the Hunger Rot that Putrifies the Flesh and Skin, and the Pelt Rot that cometh after great store of Rain to sheep new shorne, Mildewing the Skin, and Corrupting the Blood, are the most sweeping and Mortal

To prevent these then, and all others, the Danger fore seen, take the salt called Adracei, and once a Week Rub their Mouths with it, and it is a great Prevention, and Preserver of them against Rots: But if the Rot is gone amongst them, seperate late the Infected, immediatly Bleed the rest in their Ears, under the Tongue, and in the Vein between the Jaws, give them Bay-Salt, Fennel, and ash Keys Boiled in their Water, and every one of them a Brandy-Cup full or Aqua-Vitæ, sweetned with Honey.

As for the Infected, Bleed them in the Temple Veins, then take Fulsilago, Colts-Foot, and Lungwort, each an equal quantity, stamp them, and strain the Juice into Water pretty well sweetned with Honey, and early in the Morning give it them warm to drink, to each a Quarter of a Pint, and they will soon Recover, unless their Lungs be utterly perished: Feed them with short dry Hay, and Tares. The latter a little sodden in fair Water, in which Fennel has been Infused, Let their Housings be free from any Moisture, or ill Scents, and let them Lye Warm on clean dry Straw or Fernn, for a Sheep is a Nice Creature, much affecting Cleanliness, and wholsome Airs Take Care likewise to drive away all Venomous Creatures from them, and this may be done by Burning Galbanium, Hart's-Horn Shavings, or Womans Hair: You may also give them (in their Trogh) Barly and Beans Ground together, or dryed Pease and Acorns Ground, mixed with Bran, and if the Elme continues Leafy, give them the tender Boughs to Brouze on, and thus you will Preserve your own, whilst other not Regarding these Rules, will have theirs swept away by Scores, if not by whole Flocks when the Rot comes amongst them, therefore seeing you are well advised, neglect it not.

How to Calculate Nattivities, to know Good or Bad Fortune. Introducing to that curious Art, plainly describing it by the Complexions Humours, &c.

ALL the Sages and Wise-men of the World have held, and yet do hold, that the influence of the Planets, other Stars and Signs of the

Zodiack have a great Power and Force in disposing the Affairs of Men and Women, in the contingencies of their Lives, as well as to their bodily Health,

Health and Sickneſs; this granted, I proceed to ſhew you how this may be fore known, and many Incommodities prevented thereby.

Conſider firſt then to know the Day and Hour of the Birth of the Party, whoſe Nativity you would Calculate; as ſuppoſe on a Monday, at half an Hour paſt Five in the Morning, then you find the Moon has Dominion of that Birth; the Perſon ſo born will be of a pale Complexion, ſoft flaxen, or whitiſh Hair, ſubject to cold Diſeaſes, inconſtant, of no great Ca acity or Underſtanding, and in Peril of loſing his or her Life by drowning: See in this Caſe in the Scheme, the Moon aſcendant in *Gemini*, ☽ ♊ in the third Angle.

If on Tueſday, when *Mars* predominates the Perſon be born. It is diſcovered by a wide mouth, a fiery Counterance, great Lips, a high Noſe and Fore-head, threatning Eyes a ſwarthy Complexion, black or dark Hair, the Diſpoſition of that Party is Furious, given to Brawls from which much Troubles ariſes, and in the End Danger of Life, ſeldom attaining to extreme old Age ſee his Character in the ſecond Angle thus, ♂ ♌

If on Wedneſday, at any Hour under the Dominion, is under *Mercury* and their the Party has a little Noſe, a bright, browniſh or red Hair, a little Mouth quick ſparkling Eyes, a flat Fore-head, and little Head, ſubject to much talking, a lover of Company, ſubtil deceitful, and by ill Practices frequently threatned with an untimely Death, by entring on Plots and Stratagems, obnoxious to great Ones, his Character is thus to be known, ☿.

If born of a Thurſday, *Jupiter* predominates, and you find his Character in the ſecond Angle, thus ♈ aſcendant in *Leo*, the ♌ Party born under

this

this Constellation, is of a ruddy, fair, and sanguine complexion, a high Forehead, but of a round plump Visage, a little enclining to an oval, the Nose in differently standing forth, the Hair a lovely brown, or enclining to lightish, the Eyes hazle, but of a cheerful Aspect, his or her behaviour is cheerful, full of obligement, true to trust, and a good Friend, his or her Fortune will rise by the Help of great Ones, and his Sicknesses, which will not be many, proceed from over abundance of Blood, causing Fevers and the like; a long Life, and much Riches is promised to those under this Influence.

Those born on a Friday, under the Dominion of *Venus*, whose Character stands thus ♀ in the depressed, or undermost Angle of the Body, or Point of the Scheme, in *Taurus* ♉ the Person born under her Influence, is of a fair Complexion, flaxen Hair, and many times bright, enclining to red, affable of Temper, black sparkling Eyes, dimpled a little in the Cheek or Chin, fortunate by Marriage, and greatly beloved, many Children in Wedlock; and others without it, yet often afflicted with hot Diseases, and very old Age is not promised but Danger threatned of Mortal Wounds, in lustful Contentions.

If from under *Saturn*'s Dominion that is on Saturday, whose Character is thus, ♄ in the fourth Angle, opposite to *Taurus* ♉ and *Leo* ♌ deprest, the Party will in this case have red or dusky Hair, a sallow or meloncholy Complexion, slow to Speech, blue Eyes, a long Visage, and strait Mouth, subject to Melancholy secret Revenge, studious and thoughtful, no Riches is promised, but Afflictions and Trouble; wise and prudent, but Unfortunate in undertakings, wear out a long and troublesome Life.

If

If born under the Sun, Charactered thus, ☉ in the sixth Angle, in the Sign *Aries*, ♈ the Party will be of a cheerful Countenance, a ruddy Complexion, enclining a little dusky, of a Humour affable, and very Fortunate by a Favour

How to tell any Number one shall think, be it never so great.

THis is a pretty Device, and some have been thought to Conjure, or Divine, when they did so exactly know the Thoughts of others, *&c.* and it is no more than this: When the Party has Thought of any Number, bid him or her Multiply the Number thought, by Five, and give you the product, by which Means the Number thought will be so far above that thought on, that he will never scruple it, concluding it is impossible to Reduce it, and this Product being infallibly a Five, or a Cypher, then take away the Number thought on will remain

As suppose the Thought Number were 53, which doubled, produce 106, and this Multiplied by 5, is 530. The Cypher then taken away, it is 53, the Number Thought on: And thus you may do (observing this Rule) by what Number soever any One shall cast in their Mind.

To know the Planet that hath Dominion in the Nativity of any Person.

THis a very nice Point, yet conducing to abundance of Advantage, in knowing what shall befal one in the Course of Life, for as the Planets Good or Bad, so our Fortune will be; but be-

before I give further Directions, obſerve the following Alphabetical Table, with their agreeing Figures

1	2	3	4	5	6	7	8
A	B	C	D	E	F	G	H
9	0	20	0	4	50	60	70
I	K	L	M	N	O	P	Q
10	0	100	200	300	400	500	
R	S	T	V	X	Y	Z	

In this Caſe take the Number of every Letter of the Chriſtian Names of the Party enquiring, and the like of their Parents Names, apply them to the Letters of the Table, and their Figures, then bring the ſeveral Numbers into one Sum Total, then divide by 9, and then 1 or 4 remains, it Denotes the Sun to have Domination in the Nativity, promiſing long Life, Riches, and Honour. If 7 or 2 then its the Moon, and your Life will be inconſtant and changeable: If 9, *Mars*, promiſing a troubleſome Life by reaſon of Jarrs, Strife, and a reſtleſs Spirit: If 5, *Mercury*, denoting the getting of Wealth, but not the Art of keeping it, unſtable, deceitful, *&c.* If 3, *Jupiter*, promiſing Riches, and Favour of great Ones. If 6, *Venus*, promiſing in Love ſucceſsful: If 8, *Saturn*, bringing a ſullen-bad Fortune.

The Art of diſcovering Truth from Falſehood.

IF you ſuſpect you take a Servant, or any other in a Lie or falſe Story, that may be to your prejudice

judice, or otherways, be no presently so rash as to Change them with it, but try the following Rule of Art, to inform you a certainty, of what you can but at present surmize or suspect, without any real Ground. W[illegible] the Parties Name, and the Name of the Day the Discourse was, or is made on, that you cannot h[illegible]ve and then mind the following Alphabet and Figures.

A	B	C	D	[illegible]	F	G	H
10	2	20	4	14	6	16	7
I	K	L	M	N	O	P	Q
28	11	11	12	4	14	6	16
R	S	T	V	X	Y	Z	
18	18	10	2	2	4	14	

Take the Letters and Figures properly belonging to them, as the Letters make the Name of the Party suspected, also add those of the Nature of the Day, and when you have put them into a Sum Total, add 26, then by 7 divide the Sum Total, and then take the Remainder, and if it proves odd, you may be confident the Party has told you an Untruth or *Æsop's Fables,* instead of a *Veracity.* But if even you may rely upon what he or she has said, and in Case of an Untruth, you may positively Charge the Party with it, and either by an open Confession, Blushes, or some evident Signs, you may easily come to the Knowledge how you had like to have been deceived.

How

How to know whether you shall be Successful in any Matter you Engage in against another.

IF you would know whether you shall have the Advantage against your Adversary, in any Matter of Controversie, as a Suit of Law, Love, Raceing, Gameing, Bargaining, or the like; *to do this*, consider the Name of each Party, and rarely they happen alike, having well considered them, set down the following Alphabet (with Figures) under the Letters, *viz*

A	B	C	D	E	F	G	H
13	3	22	24	22	3	7	6
I	K	L	M	N	O	P	Q
20	1	10	33	13	8	13	7
R	S	T	V	X	Y	Z	
13	9	8	2	6	6	4	

And now to amaze the Party more that comes to be resolved, put the Christian Names into *Latin*, in the *Nominative Case Singular*, as suppose *Peter* is contending, or to contend in any of these Matters with *Paul*, set down *Petruus* & *Paulus*, and so of any other Name, then according as the Alphabet directs, joyn unto every Letter of the Name proposed, the Figure or Figures under the Letter, as they stand in Order, then cast up the Numbers to each Party by itself, and being put together, proceed to Divide by 9, and so.

so doubt not to find the Division being made what Remains to the one Party, and to the other; and this gives a Sight to the Victor, and the Vanquished; and if it so happen, that in the Division of the whole 9, nothing remains, then take the last Number of 9, to serve for your purpose. As I shall more fully explain in the Close: And thus I begin with the Name mentioned, as by the same Rule you may do with any other.

P 13			☽	*P* 13		
E 22	67	*makes seven*	☿	*A* 1	37	*makes four*
T 8		*times Nine.*	♂	*U* 2		*times Nine*
R 13			☉	*L* 10		
U 2			♄	*U* 2		
' 9		*Remains* 4.	♃	*S* 9		*Remains* 1.
Sum 67						*Sum* 37

And by this Rule, the Planets give their favourable Influence to *Peter*, and promise him the Advantage over the other, as having 4 to 1, against him in the Remainder, that is, three odds to give him a good Lot: But yet to make this more Manifest, take the following Table according to the fore going Rule.

1		3	5	7	9
2	———	1	4	0	8
3		2	5	7	9
4	He that shall	1	3	6	8
5	Overcome is of	2	4	7	9
6		1	3	5	8
7	———	2	4	6	8
8		1	3	5	7
		2	4	6	8

And thus you may know what is proper without any Frivolous Conceits of Conjuration, or dealing with the Black Art to Injure or Hurt your self by Diabolical Charms or Enchantments.

To know whether the Party you Love be Virtuous and Chaste.

THis is a nice Secret, and may do much Good in preventing much Evil and Strife after Marriage, Write down the proper Name of the Party, either Man or Woman, with his or her Mothers Name, and put the Number to each Letter, as the fore-going Experiment, add 15 to the Sum Total, divide it then by 9, and so the Sum remaining, the Remainder of that Sum being even, then conclude the Person Chaste, Honest, and Virtuous; but if it appear odd, then you may with all imaginable Reason, conclude the Contrary.

The Mosaick Wand to find out hidden Treasure.

THis has been a Secret put in Practice to great Advantage, in this Order; Cut a Hazle-wand forked, at the upper end like a Y, Peel off the Rhine, and dry it in a moderate Heat, then steep it in the Juice of Wake Robin, or Night Shade, and cut the single lower End sharp, and where you suppose any rich Mine, or hidden Treasure is near, place a Piece of the same Mettal you conceive is hid, or in the Earth, to the Top of one of the Forks by a Hair or very fine silk or Thread, and do the like to the other End, pitch the sharp single End lightly to the ground, at the going down of the Sun, the Moon being in the Encrease, and in the

Morning

Morning at Sun-rise, by a Natural Sympathy) you will find the Mettal enclining, as it were pointing to the Place where the other is hid.

Choice Secrets in Astrology on several Useful Occasions.

MAny have been desirous to know (as a great Secret) the Power that is given to the Planets, and other Stars, to prevent Thefts and De-

predations on Houses, Out-houses, Orchards, Parks, Warrens, Fields of Corn, Cattle, Timber, and the like: How either to stop and take the Thief, or scare him from coming thither, and since Wonders have been wrought in this, to Secure

cure honest People in their just Rights, and it being hither to an occult Faculty, or rare Secret, I shall give the Reader such an Insight into the Matter, as few have hitherto done.

A safe Way to secure a House.

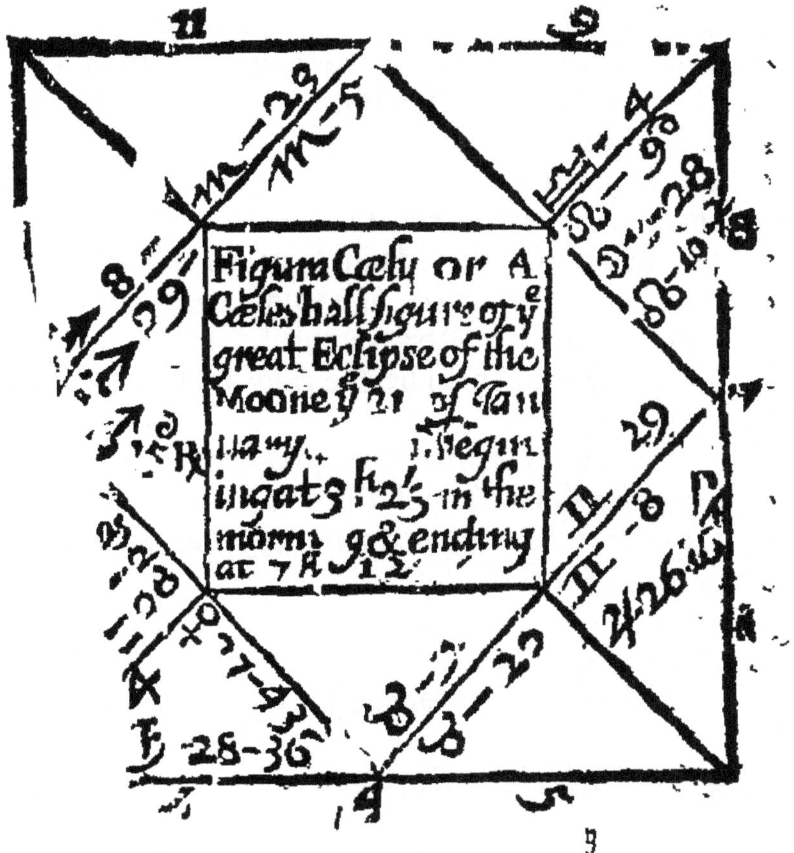

IF you suspect your House will be robbed, and would secure it from Thieves, as no doubt

but

but you are desirous, consider the Night what Planet Reigns, and is Lord of the Ascendant, and these are the Characters, the *Sun* on ☉ Sunday, the *Moon* ☽ on Monday, *Mars* ♂ on Tuesday, *Mercury* ☿ on Wednesday, *Jupiter* ♃ on Thursday, *Venus* ♀ on Friday, *Saturn* ♄ on Saturday: Now consider on what Night you do this, as to these Planets and Write on fair Parchment these Characters, ☊♈♑, and suppose it be on a Sunday, add the Planetary Character ☉ with this Number, 1, 3, 5, $\frac{1}{4}$, $\frac{1}{7}$, and at that Night, lay this under the Earth, or covered with a Tile in the Middle of the House, as near as may be, sprinkle it over with the Juice of Night Shade, and so go to sleep as soon as you have thrice repeated them over, and if the Thieves have power to enter the House, they shall have no power to get out again, or to carry any thing away till the Sun Rises, and if you be watchful, then you may easily apprehend them before they are able to depart.

And thus you may do any Day in the Week, adding the Character of the Planet that Rules that Day, as I have set it down, to what is beside set down in Order.

A Safeguard for all Out-houses to secure Poultry, Cattle, Corn, or what else is shut up therein.

CONsider the Day, as in the Former, and set down in a piece of clean Parchment these Characters, ♋♉♏ add the Character of the Planet, as for Monday ☽ and these Figures, 9, 8, 5, 3, $\frac{1}{3}$, $\frac{1}{7}$, lay this sprinkl'd with the Juice of Hemlock under

the

The Threshold of the Out-House, or if there be none, in some secret Corner, and if any Thieves Enter, they will be so Blinded and Amazed, that they will not find their way out again, but groap in vain till the Sun Rise, before which time you must be Watchful to come thither, for the Sun shooting its Beams thro' the Air, the Guardian Virtues Retire, and the Force is dissolv'd for that time, but with changing the Planet will serve for the next Night, and so on.

A Safeguard for an Orchard, Park, Warren, or Field, to take a Thief, &c.

THE several Places being Guarded by one and the same Planet, not to be too tedious to you, one and the same thing will indifferently serve to secure any of them from Thieves that come to make Robbery or Depredation, whether it be for Fruits of the Earth, or any kind of Cattle, or to steal away Timber in Fields or Woods; to make which, take the following Direction, have a piece of curious clean Parchment, made of a sleek Skin, Cut it with five Points or Corners in the form of a Star but so large, that you may Write in the Center of it, what is to be Written, *viz* ♊ ♐ ♓ the Character of the Celestial Signs Governing these Affairs, add the Caracter of the Planet for the Day, as before Directed, and suppose it to be *Tuesday, Mars* that Governs that Day has this Character, which set down thus, ♂ and this Number 1. 7. 11. 12. $\frac{1}{2}$ $\frac{1}{8}$. close it up with Virgins Wax, as I should have told you, you ought to have done the former, and sprinkle it with the Juice of Fumitory, and place the same (if in a Garden) in the Hole of a Wall, if in a Field, Forest, Park, or Wood, in the Hole of a Tree, having laid it before in Goose Tansey, and so whatever any Thief takes in these several Grounds, he shall not be able to carry off till the Sun rising; but then if not watched he may do it.

To drive away Ghosts or Spirits that haunt a House, and prevent the night Mare.

THis is a curious Secret, and I think never before made publick, or privately practised, but by a few: *To do this, take the Wool that* grows between the two Eyes of a black Sheep, burn it to Powder, and after it has been steeped a Night and a Day in Man's Urine, mix this with the Powder of Nightshade, or Wake *Robin*, an Herb so called, boil them in a Quarter of a Pint of *Aqua Vitæ*, sprinkle the Walls of the Chamber you fancy is haunted with it, and no Disturbance will happen if you turn your Face when you go to repose, to the *Eastward*, when in Bed, and say your Prayers.

This to be carried about One, for the prevention of Witchcraft, being under an ill Tongue, or Planet struck.

THese Misfortunes generally happen under the Power of the Moon, who (as Ancients hold) is the Favourer of the Magick, or Enchantment, take the most Opposite Planet to her in allaying

laying her Force this way, which is *Jupiter*, write his Character thus ♃ on a Piece of Parchment, and add to it the following Characters, that are the Signs of the *Zodiack*, viz. ♍♎♏ and this Number, 1, 3, 7, 5, 7. $\frac{1}{-}$ $\frac{1}{7}$ $\frac{1}{4}$, after this, set down the Number the Figurative Letters in your Name make, wrap it up in as small a Compass as you can, and sowing it up in a Piece of black Silk, that has been steeped in the Juice of Virvine, hang it about your Neck, when the Moon changes, and you will be secure from any Danger of this Nature, if you lead a good Life.

To prevent affrightning Dreams, and take away Fear in the Night.

YOu must take *Laudanum* a dram, Frankincense the like quantity, of *Bezora* stone as much, beat these into Powder, and write upon a Piece of Parchment these Characters ♄ ♃ ♉ ☿, and under them your Name; put the Powder in the Paper you write on, and when you repose, bind them on your Forehead and Stomach, for you must have two Papers order'd one and the same Way, as directed, putting half the Powder in the One, and the other half in the Other.

To help a Person under an ill Tongue, and make the Witch appear or the Effect cease

CUT off some of the Parties Hair, just at the Nape of the Neck, clip it small and burn it to Powder, put the Powder in Salt Armoniack, write the Parties Name you suspect backwards, and put the Paper clipt in *Aqua Vitæ* into the other Two, then set it over a gentle Fire; let the

 Party

Party afflicted sit by it, and diligently watch it, that it run not over to catch flame, speaking no Word, whatsoever Noise is heard, but take Notice of what Voice or Roaring is heard in the Chimney, or any part of the Room, and then write how often you hear it, and fix before each writing this Character, ☽ and if the Party who Afflicts you, appears not visible, though you may know the Voice, repeat it again, and if she appear in no visible shape, it may make her Charm impotent, and give Relief to the Afflicted Party.

To prevent or take Vermine, that come to destroy Poultry, or Coney Warrens.

YOU must take a piece of a Woolf's skin, the Hair on, the breadth of the palm of your hand, or somewhat more, prick a great many holes in it with a bodkin, in the three corners, but leave the middle intire, scrape the middle part to the fleshy side, so that it may be smooth enough to write on, then write these Characters 2. 3 4 7 5. this done, write the Guardian △ ⊕ Λ II L Name underneath them, *viz Azmeros,* then burn the Wool of Foxes-tail, with some Featherfew, and the Seed of Henbane, lay the Powder on the Characters, that it may cover them pretty well, then fold the corners, and stitch them up close with the Powder in it, and this done, sprinkle it with the juice of Hysop, and hang it up with a couple of Horse hairs drawn out of the middle of the Tail of a live Stone-Horse, and hang it up in your Hen-House, Dove Cot, or for a Warren, on a pole, or a Tree, as near as you can in the middle of the Coney Burrows, and the Vermine will either fear to ap-

proach

proach, scenting it at a distance, or being come near it, will continue snuffing, and endeavouring to get at it, then you may come and destroy them with a Gun, Dogs, Cross-bow or otherways as you find most practicable, instead of a Woolf's skin, you may use a Badgers, if the other cannot be had.

To prevent a Dog barking at you in the Night-time.

YOU must take the Skin off the Forehead of an Hyena, a Beast so called, which may be had at the Furriers Shop, boil it in the Urine of a young Stone Colt, and smoak it over the burnt Hoof of a Cow, twice or thrice, till it is dry and so carry it about you, and so long as you do this, where ever you come in the Night, the Dogs will not only be silent, but run away from you as fast as they can, when you approach any thing near them For if they once Scent it (as certainly they will) the great aversion they have to it, will make them tremble, and avoid you, without being able to open at you.

To draw Cats together, so that they shall not escape your Hands.

SO soon as ever the new Moon appears, gather the Herb Nepe, and dry it a little in the heat of the Sun. When it is temperately hot, then take a fair piece of Parchment, and cut it in the shape of a half Moon, write on it these Characters ☿ ♄ ✶ wrap the Parchment up close, and put it amongst the Herb which hang up in a Net, in a convenient place, and when one of them has scented it, her

Cry will soon call all those about her, that are within hearing, and there they will rage and run about leaping and capering, to get at the Net, which must be so hung, or placed, that they cannot easily do, for they will certainly tear it to pieces, and in this you will have pleasant Pastime, as well as to take and destroy them if they are offensive to your Gardens, Houses, Dove-cots, &c.

A Pledget to wear about ones Neck, to prevent Bugs, Fleas, or Gnats biting in the Night-time.

THis to many People may prove no less advantagous than any, especially where these Insects are a second Plague of *Egypt* to People. To do this, Gather Asmart or Hounds Tongue, an Herb with a long sharp pointed little Leaf that grow in Ditches, in moist places in Summer, dry it to a Powder, add it to as much of the powder of Sarsafax Wood, as will lye upon a Shilling, sprinkle them a little with Juniper Water, mix it with the Wool of a black Sheep, cut off betwixt the Horns, in the Wain of the Moon, write on a peice of paper these Characters ♒ ♂ ♏ ✱ ♄ $\frac{1}{2}$ $\frac{1}{3}$ Sprinkle the Paper, when you have folded it up, with the Juice of Rue, and sew it up in a thin silk Bag, and with a little small Cats-guts hang it about your Neck, when you go to sleep, and if you are awake the power is the same; you will Rest without being disturbed with these, or other Insects.

To drive away Mice or Rats, in a House or Granery

IF you can get a he Weasel about the Increase of the Moon kill him, and take out his Fat, then dry his Skin, that you may write on the fleshy side of it, these Characters, ♉ ♈ ♊ ♋ ☾ ✱, do it over with Weasels Fat, and stuff up the Skin with Moss, taken from the Root, or lower part of an Oak-tree, and place it on a sharp Haw-thorn-stick, put the sharp end into it Bellywards, and stick the other End in the Floor, in a little hole made with a Gimblet in the place of their resort, let it not be placed more than six Inches above the Floor, and as many as come there, will immediately avoid the House, or Out-house, and if you would kill them there, it is but strewing Pot ashes on the Floor, and it will work so powerful, that they cannot get away; but there you may kill them at pleasure.

To prevent being robbed on the Road, or meeting with any bad Accident.

COnsider (in this Case) what Planet you set out under, ruling as to the Days, and its influence: The Moon ruling *Monday*, denotes inconstancy in Success *Mars Tuesday*, violence *Mercury* on *Wednesday* deceit and fraud: *Saturn* on *Saturday*, envy, and malignamnity: But the *Sun*, *Jupiter* and *Venus*, governing *Sunday*, *Thursday* and *Friday*, are very friendly Planets, promising Success. However, other Days are proper enough, with the Cautions I shall give you hereafter, and this is as followeth, to prosper, and per-

prevent ill Fortune, in being Robbed, Falling from your Horse, or Sick, falling into any Pit, Water, or the like.

Now Note, That the Malignant Planets are friendly to others, and befriended of them again; *Sol* is friendly to *Jupiter*, and *Venus*, *Luna* to *Jupiter*, *Venus* and *Saturn*, *Mars* is friendly to *Venus*, *Mecury* is friendly to *Jupiter*, *Venus*, and *Saturn*. *Jupiter* is friendly to *Sol Luna Mercury Venus* and *Saturn*; *Venus* is friendly to *Sol*, *Luna*, *Mars*, *Mercury*, and *Jupiter*, *Saturn* is friendly to *Jupiter*, *Sol*, and *Luna*. And these are temporizing to hinder the Malignancy of each other, therefore the Promises considered, now as to what you are to put in Practice for your Security.

Gather Veruin, an Herb so called, in the new of the Moon hang it up in the Chimney to dry, then powder it, and steep it in the water of *Agaus Castus*, then dry it again, and reduce it to fine Powder; these temporize with the Planets *Venus* and *Mercury*, which are so powerful in their Influence for the protection of Travellers: Put this Powder into a Hollow Ring, of any kind of Mettle and have these Characters engraved on the inside, of it, ♀ ☿ ♄ then you may go or ride safe without danger of any violence, keeping your Mind on Good Things

To find out a Thief, or make him or her bring back the Goods stolen.

YOU must set down the day, hour, and minute, if you can, when the Goods were stolen, and the name of the Planet ruling the day, as I have before set down, to direct you. This being done, set down these following Characters, in a fair piece of Parchment ☾ ⁂ ♄ ✱ △ ☿ this done, turn Round thrice, and if you hear no News in 44 Hours of the Thief, as ten to one you will, then prick the Parchment full of Holes, and hang it up in the Chimney, where the Heat of the Fire may a little Scorch it, and the Thief is held to be so restless in his Mind, and tormented that he or she will discover the Thief to be at Ease, or bringing Home your Goods, throw them privately into your House, or some Place appertaining to you

A pleasant Device or Stratagem to find out any Person suspected to have Robbed you.

IF you suspect a Servant, or any other, not being Positive, you may first (to Amuse them) threaten to send for the Cunning-Man, to know by his Art what is become of the Things lost, and soon after have a Stranger come unknown to them and order the Party you suspect, with some others for Company to come into a Room, being Ignorant of what is Intended, then the Stranger Whelming a Kettle very Sooty or Black at Bottom muttering hard Words, the Room must be made quite Dark, then he must bid them walk three times round the Kettle, Hand in Hand; then suddenly say, *Lay each of you your Hand upon the Kettle, as hard as you can*, and when he that has stole the Goods, comes to do it, for it must be done in Turns; one after another, the Cock will Crow, and Discover him or her, those that are Innocent will do it without Scruple; but the Guilty Person, if he be Ignorant of the Trick, being in the Dark, will Refuse it, because it cannot be seen whether he does it is not, and when they a'l say they have done it, asking them severally over, the party must begin to admire the Cock crows not, for you must not expect he will do it upon this Account, unless by chance, and say, He believe the Party is not here that has stolen the Goods, when making all Light again, he must require to see their Hands, to be more perfectly Instructed in the Matter and then, by then if any of their Hands are not smutted, or have no Mark of Blackness, it is plain that Party has not touched the Kettle, and then being home charged with the Matter, he will doubtless confess it, and the reason he declined it, by which Means you may come by your Goods again, if they have not been so long lost, that they are altogether wasted or embezelled.

To know what Place is best to Live and Thrive in, whether one shall be Rich or Poor, &c

ONE considerable Thing has been desired by many, and that is to know the places where they may thrive best, of the Employment destined by the Heavenly Constellations, whereby they may best thrive in the World: This is to be considered, by the Constellation, or Planet the Party is born under, and the Sign in which at that time it is, which gives the Influence in Affairs of Life and Note that the Moon passes thro' the twelve Signs of the *Zodiack* in 28 Days, some odd Hours and Minutes, and by observing the Birth whilst she is in these several Signs, the following Conjectures are to be made.

If in *Aries* or *Taurus*, thus Characted, ♈ ♉, the party shall thrive best in Inland Countries, managing rural Affairs, as Breeding Cattle, tilling

Tilling Ground, Planting Fruit Trees, leading a happy contented Life, amidst great Plenty and encrease, and live to a good Old Age, have many Children.

If the Sun be in Gemini at the Nativity, thus Charactered ♊ then shall there be great Advantages by Marriages, and in populous Towns or Cities is the best place of Living, Dealing in Crafts, or Working in Manufactures but Sickness will happen, and a Victorious Old Age hardly be obtained. If the Moon be in Cancer, thus charactered ♋ the Party shall deal in Minereals to thrive best, or Silver, Brass, Copper, Tin, Lead, or Iron, and Gain much by the Crafts and Trades they are properly used in, Working in Fire, or else Profess Chymistry, or Alchamy, and Cities or other great Places of Traffick, are the best to Settle in for Thriving, and growing Rich, tho' at the first the Party will not fail to meet with great Misfortunes and Disencouragement, however be not Disheartned, they will blow over and a more Prosperous Sceen appear, yet will the Party Born so be troubled with Hot Diseases, as Fevers, continual Intermitting Fevers Epylepsies, Fluxes, *&c.*

If the Moon be in Leo, when the Nativity happens, it is thus Charactered ♌ it betokens the Party stout, Generous, and Born to great Fortune, rising by the Favour of Princes, and great Men. If a Male, Heroick and Valiant Actions shall get him Fame and Renown, if a Female, she shall have Honourable Marriages, but neither of their Lives are promised to continue to Old Age, by reason they will be of a dry Constitution, the most Thriving Place to Live in, will be near Princes Courts, the House of Great Men in populous Towns or City, or

Travelling

Travelling in Foreign Countries to get Fame and Riches.

If the Moon be in *Virgo*, at the time of the Nativity, it denotes the Man or Woman shall be loving, affable, and of a winning Behaviour, gaining the Love of all, have Encrease of beautiful Children, though to Women, it denotes Pains and Peril in Child Birth. The best way to thrive is by Manual Occupation, Manufactures in Linnen, Wollen and the like, but they will be troubled with Phlegmetick Diseases, as Colds, Coughs, Consumption, Dropseys, Rheumatisms, and the like, coveting a Country Life, where it is Allotted for Persons Born under the Cælestial Sign, and Dominion of the Moon, best to Thrive, however they shall live long, but get no great store of Wealth. This Sign is thus Charactered, ♍

If the Nativity fall in the Moon's Ingress to *Libra*, thus Charactered ♎ the Party shall best thrive in Cities, or Towns, by Selling Trades, or Merchandize, dealing much in Wares, and growing Rich thereby, of a temperate moderate Constitution, not over scraping, or covetous of Riches, though much Plenty shall be gotten by Industry, the Diseases that attend such Persons, shall be indifferently mixed, sometimes Hot, at other times Cold, and they are promised mostly to see a middle Age, with Comfort of many Children.

If the Nativity falls out when the Moon is in the Sign *Scorpio*, thus Charactered ♏ the Party shall have but an indifferent being, forced to move from place to place, by reason of malicious Enemies, and be in danger to Die at last by Poison, or some Malignant Infection.

If the Moon be in *Sagatarius*, thus Charact-

ered

ered ♐ near Woods and Forrests is the properest
place to Live in, the Party shall be much delight-
ed in Hunting, Shooting, be very Hardy, Dex-
terous, and Ingenious in Understanding, and the
Trust Reposed, whereby the Party shall gain Fa-
vour, and be advanced, either in Service or Mar-
riage, but in the End shall be in Danger of Life,
if not Die of some Wound gotten in a Quarrel,
or Privately given by some Treacherous Enemy,
or Furious Beast

If the Moon cast the Nativity of a Person in *Capricorn*, the Person shall be much given to lust-ful Desires, it is thus Charactered ♑ delighting in Rural Affairs, yet subject to Remove often from Place to Place, and not long Contented with any fixed Abode however disappointments happening at the first, the End shall be more Favourable, and Fortunate by Marriage, though no great store of Children; yet Hot and Dry Diseases will much Afflict the Party, and extream Old Age is not promised him or her Born under the Influence

If the Moon be in the Signs, *Aquarius or Pisces*, thus Charactered ♒ ♓ it denotes the Party to be of an Unstable, Roving mind, yet very Industrious given to the Desire of Travel, and to Marine Af-
fairs Thriving best to Merchandize, and delight-
ing in Sea port Towns, and Places near Great Water, most commonly Successful, gaining great Riches, but of a Phlegmatick Constitution, subject to Agues, Dropsyes, and other Distempers, occasioned by Cold and Moisture, but has a promise of long Life, though not over Fruitful in Children.

And thus may many other things be conjectured, or Gathered from this, that I have not set down: And

And to be informed when the Moon is in any of these Signs, and Predominant to compare it with the Time of Birth, for them more assurance of its Influence, it may (upon first view) be found in many common Almanacks, each Sign Governing a Solar Month, of which there are but Twelve to the Year, though of Lunar Months Thirteen.

How to resolve all lawful Questions, relating to Marriage Friendship, Journying, Life long or short, Business, Success, or any others truly stated

TO be informed in curious Questions, better than if you go to those that imprudently are called by the Vulgar, Cunning men, I shall put you into such a Method, as you will be enabled to do it your self, without Trouble or Expence of Money, or being scared or affrighted with their pretended Conjuration, being the same Rule they take, to make their Guesses, and Conjection, which often hit right. The Planet and other Stars considering in their proper Motion, Positions, Oppositions and Conjunctions, for so they have a great Influence on earthly Things, and over the Actions of Men, to dispose and order them in their Affairs, and Moderate many Matters that would otherways be violent and Destructive.

In

In Order to this I have erected a Scheme, and when you would conſider any Queſtion, to know it, firſt view well the Scheme erected, and calculated for the reſolving all lawful Queſtions. Mark how the Signs and Planets are poſited in their Government of the Cæleſtial Houſes, and then the Figures in the Square.

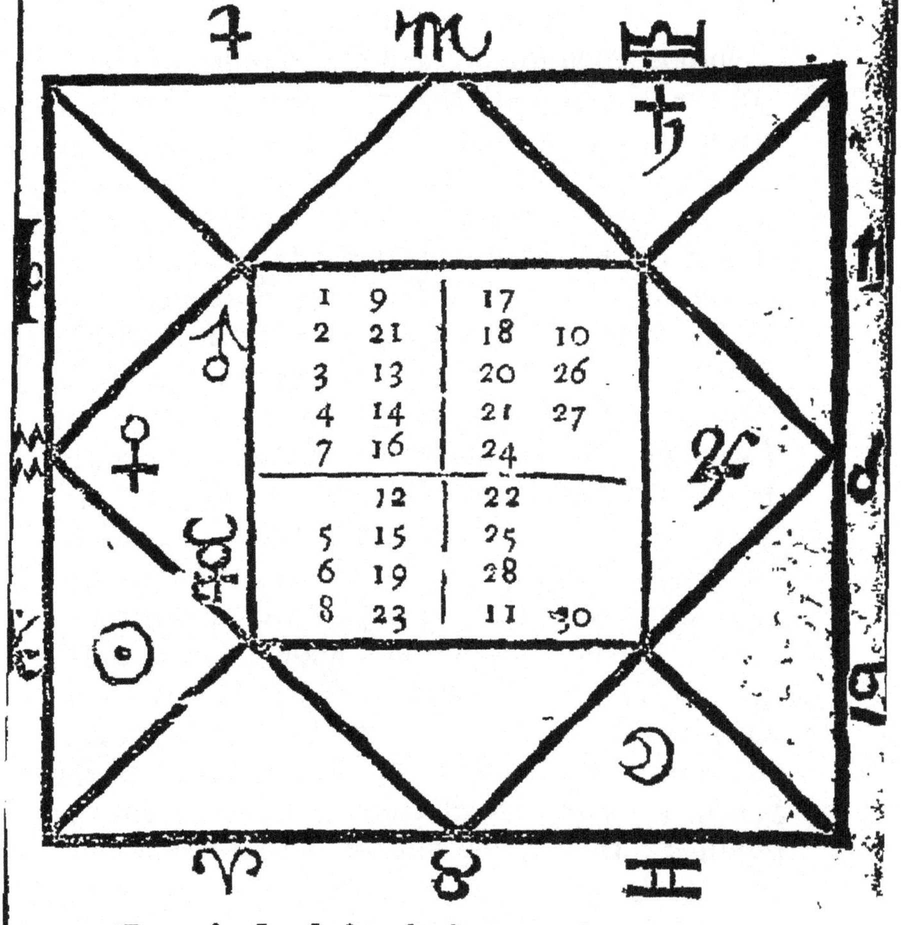

To underſtand this the better, take in the Number of the Day of the Month, and Mark what Planet Rules that Day you ſtate your Queſtion to be reſolved, and theſe are their Characters, as to the

the Governing the Days of the Week, as you find in the Angles or Houses of the Scheme Erected, on *Sunday* ☉ Governs on *Monday* ☾, on *Tuesday* ♂, on *Wednesday* ☿, on *Thursday* ♃, on *Friday* ♀, on *Saturday* ♄, this being Noted, pitch up n any Number that exceeds not 30, add to it the Number of the Day of the Month, and the Letter that begins your Name, if it be a fig ire, if it be n t, it stands but for 1, then gather the Number thought or and the Number of the Day of the Month, with that of your Name Letter, into one Sum, and divide it by 30, and then if you find what remains in the upper part of the square, in he Figures placed there assure your self of Good Luck, but if it falls out in the under part, it promises b it a i Indifferency of Fortune.

As for Examp'e, you would be certified wheth r you shall have the Party you are in Love withal, and desire to Marry, tak the Number of the first Letter of your Name, and the Number of the Planet, that Governs the Day you enquire reckoning from *Sunday*, as to the Days of the Week, till *Saturday*, in order, and then divide them by 30, and if it appears in the upper part, it promises you Success in what you desire to know, but if in the under part of the Table, you will be Crossed in your Expectation. If there remains neither under nor over, it Remains in the Blank Houses of the Scheme, where neither Good nor Bad Fortune is signified, then being put off with a Blank, you must think again, and proceed in the same order that is, as you find it above or below in the Table, and upon this Rule depend all Questions that can reasonably be thought on to be Demanded.

As Success in Love Affairs, Portions, great or small, Law Suits, Absence of Friends, whethe

Dead or Alive, or when return if ever, whether you shall gain the Preferment you desire, whether you shall escape Sickness or not, also in Wagers, Combats, Children, Child birth, overcoming Troubles good or bad Debts, true Friendship, News, or Stories, true or false, if a thing stolen be Recoverable or not, and indeed whatever your Occasion requires, as to Worldly Matters, which for Brevity sake, I here forbear to Innumerate, as being too many, and too tedious to set down in all their particulars.

When Diseases in the Bodies of Men, Women, and Children are more Immediately caused by the Influence of the seven Planets, with Astrological Remarks as to their Cure

SAturn ♄ Reigning causes Cold Diseases, as the Gout, Leprosey, Palsey, Quartan, Agues, Dropseys Catarrhs, Coughs Rheumatisms, &c.

Jupiter ♃ causes Cramps, Numbness, Inflamation of the Liver, Head Achs, Pains in the shoulders, Windiness in the Body, Sanguine Fevers and all Diseases caused of Putrefaction, the Appoplexy, Gazidiac Passions, Squincyes, &c.

Mars ♂ causes Acute Fevers, and Tertain Agues, continual Intermitting Fevers, Imposthumes Erisipelas, Carbuncles, Fistu'us, Bloody Flux, and such like hot and dry Diseases.

Sol ☉ causes Rheums in the Eyes, Coldness in the Stomach and Liver swooning Chollar Catarrhs, Pustles in the Matrix, and the like in the Lower Parts.

Venus ♀ causes Scabs, and Veneral, Diseases, Lientary Suffocation in the Womb, Sickness in the

the Stomach, from cold and moist Causes Infirmities of the Liver and Lungs &c.

Mercury ☿ causes Hoarsness and Distempers in the Senses, Impediments in Speech, and its Passions, Falling sickness, Coughs, Jaundice, Vomiting, Catarrhs, &c.

The Moon ☽ causes Palsey, Cholick, the Whites, Dropsey, Phlegmatick, Impostumes, Dissenteries, and all Diseases coming from Obstruction in the Veins.

Now having given you a Sight of what Diseases the Influence bring upon the Bodies of Men and Women, it is then Business to consider under what particular Planet each Individual was Born which may be known several Ways, treated on in this Book; and therefore I need not here give further Instructions as to that particular, but come to more general Terms, to know how the Bodies ought to be ordered, to prevent these Diseases, and herein (as one main Expedient) I recommend Temperance, moderate Bleeding, and purging in seasonable times, when a friendly Planet, opposit to the Malignancy of the Planet you was born under, has Dominion, which will much abate the Effect of their Influence, and give Nature a Power to oppose the Malevolency, which (if well heeded) may be a main prevention of danger us Sickness.

Observe also to gather all your Physick Herbs in the Hour of the friendly Planet, that temperizes, with that you are born under, and in so doing they will have more Strength, Power and Virtue to opperate in the Medicines, but neither Physick nor bleed on the 3d of *January* the 1st of *July*, the 2d of *October*, the last Day of *April*, the

the first of *August*, and the last, for Astrologers (with whom Physicians join) conclude perilous, by reason of the bad Influence then reigning, and if it change not the Distemper into another worse, i will Augment it, and put the party in great Danger of Death, if he or she in this Case be not Lucky to escape.

The Urinal Doctor, or a Astrological and Physical Observation, on Casting Urine Relating to Health and Sickness, with Caution to prevent threatned Evils.

CAsting of Urine is now become a new Trade, and many People much rely upon it, to know the Constitution of their Bodies, as to Sickness or Health, and though there is something in it, yet they many times go to ignorant pretenders, who will take their Money, and tell them a plausible Story, though they know nothing of the Matter; therefore among these many useful things, I shall give the Reader an Insight to know himself; and in this very one Thing, save him or her the Money, this whole Book fraught with so many Rarities will cost them.

First, Then if the Urine be Red, it signifies the Blood is Heated, and you must either Bleed or Allay that Heat with cooling Things to prevent Sickness.

2*d*, The Urine White, shows Rawness, and Phlegmatick Indigestions in the Stomach, which must be remedies by gentle Purges, to cleanse it, and restore lost Appetite.

3*d*, Thick and Muddy Urine betokens the Body surfeited, by over heating in Labour, Walking, or other Exercise, or by excessive Drinking and then to prevent a Fever, taking cooling Cordials.

4*th*,

4th A White and Red Setling, Gravelly, or sandy in the Urine, betokens the Stone, beginning to putrify in the Reigns or Bladder, Drink to prevent it the Juice of Parsley in Rhenish or white Wine

5th, A clear Perspicuous or Transparent Urine, shows a good Concoction, and perfect Digestion, and withal a Healthful Constitution.

6th, Bloody spots in Urine, denotes an Ulceration in the Reins, or Neck of the Bladder.

7th, The Urine Blackish, shows much a Dull Melancholy, and fore-runs some violent Diseases that often brings Death or a Long Tedious Sickness.

8th, The Urine Clammy and Sweet, denotes a Consumption of the Inner Parts, by bad Digestion.

9th, Urine of a Lead Colour, signifies the Body to be in an ill Habit (and threatens Death) without speedy Remedies Applyed

10th, Urine that has Yellow sparkles, or sediment in it shews Choller has the Predominancy, and much Afflicts the Body, threatens Fevers, and other hot Diseases, and by these kinds you may perfectly learn the state of the Body, as to Health or Sickness, present or approaching, for the Urine passing thro' those parts where the Distempers are Generating, carry a Tincture along with it of the Humours predominant, that is Encreasing or propagating the Disease, or on the contrary shows a healthful Constitution, tho' few are Skilful to discern it, which puts me in mind of a pleasant Story, *viz.* A Woman whose Husband had a Bruise by a fall down Stairs, carried his Urine to a Urine Casting Doctor, who pretended likewise to be a Conjurer, he (after shaking) seeing

ing little specks of Blood Float in it, had so much Understanding to tell her the Party had Receiv'd some Internal Hurt, the Woman agreed to this as Truth, but demanding by what means he came by it, upon this erected his Scheme, and in the mean time asked her so many Questions, that by the drift of her Discourse, he gathered he had tumbled down Stairs, the Woman not minding well what she had said (in the Consternation she was in at the hard Words she uttered) suppose he was Conjuring up the Devil to be resolved, in the Matter, to'd her own Words again in a different Stile; the Woman acknowledged it True, with some Admiration, but desired to know how many Pair of Stairs he might fall down (she had told him before where she liv'd) and he considering the Place consisted mostly of Low Buildings, answered, Two Pair, nay now (said she) you are out in your Art, he fell Three Stories I'll promise, this put our Doctor to his Trumps, when having Mused a while for an Excuse, he shook the Urinal again, and asked if there was all the Water her Husband made. No, (replied she) I spilt a little in pouring it in. O ho, did you so? (said he) why, that Woman is the Business, that made me Mistake, for there went away tne other Pair of Stairs in the Urine you spilt.

Caution against much Bleeding, and Physicking, and what necessary Rules are to be taken to supply the Defect.

THough I have often in this Book set down Rules for Health, and particularly Blood Letting, with the Times and Seasons proper (since Health is the Rarest Jewel of Life) yet for

for once let me give a Caution, that none by Ignorance, or too much Forwardness, instead of preserving, prejudice their Health

Though Physical Medicines are properly Good in their Order, and helpful to Nature, whose Hand-maid they are, to help her expel any noxious Humour that may produce a Virulent Distemper, yet over-doing may be more Injurious than under doing, therefore my Advice is, that none do Accustom themselves over-much to purging Medicines, or Blood-letting, except without them there will be some great Prejudice, or Defect in Nature, for when once the Body is often accustomed to them, they will be worse if it be not continued, which by often Repetition, must waste the Vital Spirits, as well as they carry off the bad Humours

Therefore chuse rather to take such apt things as are proper to keep the Body open and a wholsome moderate Dyet

Bread and Butter strewed with Rosemary Sage, Rue, or Scurvy grass, is an excellent preservative of Health, and in the Spring, or at other Convenient Season, Pottage with Clivers, Water-cresses, Elder-buds, Nettle tops, Brook-lime, Smallage, and such like cooling and moderate refreshing Herbs, are great Refreshers of Natures gently cooling and purging the Blood, and keep off Sickness for a long Season though the Bodies of Men and Women have before been Accustomed to them, but above all Things be Temperate in Eating and Drinking, Moderate in Labour and Exercise, for these are main Contributers to Health, and indead we need not be beholding to Outlandish Drugs, if we rightly consider we have sufficient of

our

our own, and that God in his Goodness has so ordered it, that Nature in every Place produce Remedies, suitable to the Diseases of the Climate.

How to dyet and order our Bodies, for the preservation of Health, for every Month in the Year; the most approved Rules.

IT will (among these useful Things) be highly Necessary to speak something of the Ordering of Man's Body, during the Circle of the Year, under the several Signs and Planets that Govern them, and dispose to Health or Sickness, more at one Time than another. The first part of the Year, that is from the 25th of *December*, till the 15th of *March*, is under *Capricornus*, *Aquarius* and *Pisces*, Signs partly Moist, and partly Dry, and those born under them, are subject to Diseases of that Nature Therefore from

DECEMBER to the End of the Month.

Take wholsome Dyet, and neither Eat nor Drink immoderately, for fear of Fluxes, Rhumatisms, Catarrhs or Husky Dry Coughs, that waste and consume the Lungs; let not Blood, unless in great Necessity, then do it moderately, and keep very Warm, rather Bleed often, if Necessity require it, then to much at once lest the Veins filling with Cold Air, causes dangerous Diseases, and in this, as in all the following Months, take care not to Bleed or Purge on the Unfortunate Days, which are set down in this Book, properly for every Month; let your purging be Gentle, and take great Care of Catching Cold.

In

In JANUARY

If the Weather be open (Necessity requiring it) Bleed Moderately, as in the former Month, but if hard Frosts set in, forbear it if posible, and Chear up your Spirits with Wine, and Cordials, but not to any Excess taking them (for the most part) in a Morning Fasting and be Temperate in Dyet, with Moderate purgations if Necessity require it, and so shall you (with God's Blessings) prevent and escape Sickness, observing the Critical Days.

In FEBRUARY.

You may this Month, if there be no hard Frost, be more bolder in Bleeding than before, but not over much, purge gently, with purging Aloes, and other purging Drinks, and in the Morning Fasting Eat warm Broaths, into which such wholsom Herbs as the Season affords have been shred, which will purify the Blood, Cooling and Refreshing the Body to prepare it for a Healthful Constitution in the Spring, and keeping off such Diseases, as then are Rife Abroad.

In MARCH.

This Month brings in the Vernal Equinox, and from the 25*th* of this Month, to the 24*th* of *June*, the Signs Aries, *Taurus*, and *Gemini*, Govern, and Produce Moist and Hot Diseases, or Agues, Fevers, Dropsies, Dissentrys, Fluxes, and the like. In this Month therefore, to keep your Body in good Condition, throughout the Quarter, Bleed

Bleed freely, if you are of a sanguine Complexion, and the Veins full of Blood, having moderately purg'd, 3 or 4 Days before, to stir the Humours, that the more Gross and Noxious may the better be carried off, and for a Week after take a Drink about a Quarter of a Pint in a Morning Warm, made of Figgs, Raisins, Liquorish, and a little Cardus, Boiled in Ale, and strained well; so you will prevent Agues, and Fevers and other Diseases Incident to this Month.

In APRIL

This is the most proper Month to Bleed and Purge in, but do it when the Air is dry and serene, so shall Head-Achs, Pain in the Eyes, Sore-Throats, and Diziness with their Concomitants, be prevented; Eat wholesome Warm Broths, but not too much of Raw Herbs; lest you are Afflicted with pains in the Stomach, and in Bleeding, Purging, and other weighty Matters, observe to avoid the Bad Days that are Perilous to Health and Business, as I before have set down.

In MAY

In this Month walk abroad Early in the Fields for your Health sake, but not Fasting, nor upon too full Stomach, Bleed as you see Occasion, if you have not been Blooded in the foregoing Month; Eat wholesome Warm Meats, pretty freely, and if the Weather be Seasonably Warm, Bathe in Clear water, but if your health permit not, then you may do it in Warm Water at Home, in which Mallows, Chamomil, and Groundsil have been boiled, and it will much refresh and strengthen the Body, purge with Senna, Rhubarb, or such like Harmless Refreshing Purgations, to Cleanse the Stomach, Liver and Lungs, and so prevent Distempers in the hotter Season; Eat not raw Trash, for Fear of a Flux, or pains in the Bowels keep to a wholesome Dyet, and take such Cordials Fasting, as may strengthen the Heart, and keep out pestilental Infectious Airs, &c.

In JUNE

In this Month be sparing of blood letting unless it be upon urgent Necessity, now Drink purging Waters (Morning and Evening) to Cleanse the Stomach and Bowels, *and keep the Body* Cool and Temperate But drink not hot Liquors upon it, lest the two struggling Opposits throw you into a Fever, or Surfeit, or cause breaking Out, with troublesome Stories, be Temperate in Meats and Drinks

In JULY.

Refrain this Month from any Violent Exercise, because the Humours are much stirred, and the Blood is apt to be put into a Ferment; Bleed not but upon great Necessity. Bath often, and Rise early in the Morning to take the fresh Air. but be not much abroad in the Heat of the Day, Eat, Cooling Things, but not over much.

In AUGUST.

Bleed not this Month, because of the Canicular or Dog-days, unless Necessity Uurge it and then but a little; forbear Eating much Green Herbs or Fruits, Drink Cooling Purging Waters, Ales, or such Liquors in the Morning, and sleep not over much, and forbear Purging till the next Month.

In

In SEPTEMBER.

I should have told you (according to my Method) that from the 24*th* of *June*, to the 25*th* of this Month, that the Signs *Cancer*, *Leo*, and *Virgo*, are Predominant, which are Hot and Dry, and suitable Diseases attended them, as the Small Pox, Fevers, Squincys, Spotted Fevers; and sometimes the Plague: Therefore it is very proper to be very Cautious, as I have hinted, in Temperate Dyet, Bleeding Physicking and the like, however, you may Eat (this Month) Cooling Fruits, yet with Moderation. Now Purge, and Bleed, that the Body Evacuted so of bad Humours, may be the better Enable to hold out against Winter Diseases, as Dropsy, Palsy, Falling Evils, and sometimes Phransy, and other Defects in the Head and Brain. Sweat Moderately: And Walk much when the Weather is Fair The Signs that Rule from the 25*th* of this Month, the rest of the Year not already mentioned, are *Libra*, *Scorpio*, and *Sagitarus*, and they are Cold, Moist, and Dry: Their Attendant Distempers are Dropsys, Rheumatisms, Cold Catarrhs, Coughs, Defects in the Lungs, and affliction of the Brain, also of the Nerves and Sinews, Pains in the Joynts, &c.

In OCTOBER

DrinkCordials (Fasting in the Morning) or good Wine, Eat Temperately Forbear Bleeding, unless some Uneasiness of your Body oblidge you to it, and then do it on the Lucky Days, when the Sign is well Posited, that it is neither in the Head, Neck, Shoulder nor Arms. Eat wholesome Diet, and not be late abroad in Foggy Unhealthy Airs.

In NOVEMBER

Go not abroad if you can help it, in Wet Drisling Days or Nights, Bleed not but for Necessity, and then but a little, for the Blood and Humours are necessary to fortify the Body against the ensuing Colds Eat Seasonably, and Temperatly, and avoid being Abroad in Foggy Mornings, above all Things Hurtful to the Lungs.

In DECEMBER.

Take care to keep good Fires, and wholesome Diet: Bleed not at all, take Caudles, strengthening Broaths, and Chear your Heart with a Glass of Wine, Humming Ale, Beer or Cyder, or any good warm refreshing Liquor, as you can come by it, Forbear much going abroad, unless in a clear Day, when the Foggs and Damps are sucked up, or dispersed by the Sun, especially if you be not of a very Healthful Constitution: And thus you may (in a great measure) keep yourself free from all Griefs and Sickness, and preserve a Healthful Constitution to extream Old Age, as in the following Lines are Described by the Poet:

Nature is Kind, if we her Rules Obey,
And stubbornly don't throw our Health away,
'Tis Life's Chief Jewel, yet we may find,
When they possess it, do it little mind:
But when 'tis gone, O what they then would (give,
That Temperately they had been wise to Live.

Of B E E S.

A Treatise of Bees, how to Order, Preserve, Swarm Gather their Honey, and all other Matters relating to them.

THE Bee, tho' a Creature Numbred among Insects, is exceeding useful to Man, their Wax and Honey being Commodities, Trafficable in all Nations; yet they are a Nice, Choice Creature, and without much Diligence and Care, cannot be brought to any extraordinary Perfection, to the Profit and Advantage of the Owners, which being proper to this Understanding (for the general good) I shall for the Instruction of those that are Ignorant in it, lay down Choice Rules and Directions how they should be Ordered to Preserve and Encrease their Stocks, that so in a little time they may turn to the great Profit of the Owners.

First, In the Choice of your Stocks, see they be Little, Lively, and Smooth: for those that are Rough and Unsightly will never prove well; above all, if you can see the Master Bee, or King, consider if he be Long and Shining, bedashed with Golden Spots, and Chearful; for on him mainly depends the Welfare of the whole Stock: for if he be Rough, Drooping, and Sluggish, the Rest will be Discouraged, Loyter, and never Work Cheartully to fill their Combs.

Secondly, Observe the Swarm be Whole and Great, which you may know by looking into the Hive, or observing great numbers clustering about the Mouth of it, but if this way fail, put your Mouth to the Mouth of the Hive, and Blow in, and if you are Anſwered by a great Humming Noiſe, then it is a full Shock, but with a little Faint one, then but a weak thin Shock.

Thirdly, Beware how you Tranſport them far, for the Change of the Air frequently Incommodes them; and if you cannot avoid this, to Remedy it, place the Hives on convenient Stools, in pleaſant Gardens, and ſcatter ſweet ſmelling, and wholeſome Herbs, and Flowers, about their Hives, in Removing, beware of Joſling for that diſorders their Combs, and puts them ſo out of Humour that they will ſcarcely ſtay where you place them, to carry them in Sheets on Poles, croſs Mens Shoulders, is the eaſieſt Way; the beſt time to remove them is in *April*, and let the place you remove them to be as like that in Situation you Remove them from, as may be; and upon a Remove, open them not in the Day time, that ſo reſting in the Night, they may ſettle themſelves, and finding their Hives open the next Morning go the quieter to Work: However, for two or three days obſerve them, that finding themſelves in a Strange Place, they take not Wing and leave you, for if they all go out of the Hive, it is an ill Sign they are gadding.

Fourthly, In placing your Bees, obſerve it be ſo, That in Winter and Spring, the Face of the Hives they are to come out at, may ſtand at the Riſing Sun, and ſo order the Matter, that in Winter they be not expoſed to too much Cold, nor in Summer to too much Heat, place them (above all Things) in a Wholeſome Air, where ſuch Plants, Herbs, and Flowers are Growing near, as beſt agree with them, as Thime, Caſſia, Roſemary, Wild Marjarum, Wild Thime Saffron, Bean-Flowers, Millot, Poppys, Roſes, *&c.* As for Yew, Cornel,

Sprig-

Sprig Lawrel, Cucumber, Goards, Elms, and all bitter Herbs and Flowers are Enemies to them.

Fifthly, They thrive better on rising Ground, where the Air is free and open than in close Valleys, yet love to be near Springs of purling Waters, that are not deep, and in such places where the Sipthrow in Spary Woods that they may lye above the Water, so that if they chance to drop in, they may get out again by that Help.

Sixthly, Place their Hives in their Ranks, standing in a Yard one above the other and keep from them as much as may be, all hurtful Creatures, that destroy the Bees, or Soil their Honey, as Red-brests, Toads, Wood packars, Moths, Hornets, Lizards, Swallows, Spiders, Sparrows, Butter-flies, Snakes, Snailes, Wasps, and the like; and so profitable are these little Creatures, that if it be a reasonable Spring and Summer, their Honey may be taken three times a Year, as in some Countries it is frequently observed *viz.* The latter end of *May*, the end of *July* and the beginning of *September*, but to leave them a Winter Supply, the best is only to take in *May* and *August*, for then they rest, and live upon part of what they got in Summer; and if they want, you must be compelled to feed them, by putting gengerly in little hollow Canes or Kexes, shivering like Troughs, filled with Honey or Sugar, and Water boiled together, or they will perish (e'er they can get out to Work again) for want of Food, you may also put in for their Food bruised Raisins, Figgs Currens, or any Sweets that are Wholsome in Taste and Scent, if the Weather be open, after the 10*th* of *March*, you may let them abroad, then will they Frame New Combs, and that done, begin to Breed, then they Labour hard for their Honey. *Seventhly*

Seventhly, If the Hive, by reason of the young Brood, be overcharged which is perceiv'd by their Clustering about the Mouth of it, and the great Humming Noise within, prepare New Hives rubbed with sweet Herbs, and Watch the coming forth of the Young Fry, from 8 to 12 in the Morning, lest they take Wing and be gone: and if they refuse to come forth, with the Fume of Galbanum, you may drive the whole Stock; and if they have two Kings, they will settle separate from each other, and so Hive each by themselves; or if the Stock be decayed, you may Incorporate two Hives in one, if you Kill one of the Master Bees, else there will be continual Wars, till they Consume one another: If at any time you see them draw out to Fight, it is but casting up some Dust amongst them, and the Fray will End.

Eighthly, To know when the Combs are full, Watch if they Drive out the Drones, which is a sign, and soon after you will see them Playing about the Hive, Rejoycing and Neglecting their Work: But in no wise take the Combs before full, for that displeases the Bees.

The Warreners Instructor: Or, A Treatise of Conies, their Ordering to Preserve, and Encrease them, Diseases, and Remedies.

SInce many times (in Coney Warrens) many Misfortunes happen to this little Creature so useful to Man, I shall (in this Useful Book) set down what must needs be grateful to such as have the Care of them, that their Wool may be good, the Breed kindly, and abundantly be fat, and preserved from the Diseases Incident to them which generally are but two Kinds, *viz* Rot and Madness.

To preserve them then in the Frosty Winter, when the Snow lies much on the Ground, and they cannot well come at the Grass, or any Herbs to sustain them provide your self well with the Sprigs of Birtch, Oak, and Hazle, to scatter in the Warren, for this Bark, before the Sap be much gone out of it, is the best, not only to feed them in some Degree, but proves Physical and binding, to keep them from watry Distempers, making them also to thrive, by giving them an Appetite to such other Food, as they can get, Turnip-Tops, Peashame, with dryed Pease in the Pods, and sprinkling of Parsley is exceeding good for them for in the sharpest time of Winter, when least is to be got, they feed best, and the Reason is, because then the Frost biting the Foggy Grass, makes it sweeter and more pleasant to them, than at other times, besides the sharpness of the Air whets their Appetites.

In these Increase they are abundant, bringing forth their Young Ones every Month, usually Three or Four at a time, and sometimes more; for as soon as the Doe is Disburthened, she presently takes Buck again, and when she has Kindled conceals her Young from the Buck, as secretly as she can, lest he should destroy them, which, when they are very Young he is apt to do, but so soon as they can run about, they are out of danger. I need not tell you what profit their Furs, and Flesh bring to Man, every one (in a manner) knowing there is a great advantage by it, they are on all Hands concluded to be Creatures of much hardness, but not long Lived, they much delight to Earth themselves in a Loamy Ground, mixed with Sand for that it is very well binding, and no

Springs in it to hinder their Working or earthing themselves, for wet is a great Enemy to them, and moist Burrows, with their Dampness, or Mustiness, causes the Rot amongst them, which soon thins the Warren, by sweeping them away in great Numbers though; in a Clay mixed with a little Gravel, Exempted from such Wet or Dampness, they thrive best, and are the Largest and Fullest, fine short sweet Hay, in Winter, layed near the Mouths of their Holes, is a great comfort to them, both to preserve them from Diseases, by drying up the over much Moisture they Contract, and making them feed the better, so Exempted from Sickness: The cause of Madness is caused by Wind and Wet, which getting in great quantities into the porous parts of the Body, arises by Vapours, to the Brain, and causes a Frenzey, or Madness in the Creature, which is known by its tumbling and rowling about, when out of the Burrow, and particularly tumbling over its Head, and bouncing about in an unusual posture, and this kills many of them; therefore, when this Sign appears, apply the following Remedies, and the Distemper will cease

A Cure for Madness in Coneys.

TAke sweet Hay, cut it a little but not too short, let it be as dry as possibly you can get it, mix it with Hair-Thistle, an Herb so called, and scatter a little fine dry Bran amongst it, and lay it near their burrows, if it be in winter snowy, Weather, sweep the Ground clear where you lay it, or put it into the mouth of the Burrows lightly, so as not to stop them up, that they may come to it without coming abroad to Expose themselves in the Cold Air, and this will restore them from this Distemper.

A Cure for the Rot in Coneys.

THE other Disease Incident to those Creatures, is the Rot, the more dangerous of the two, because it sweeps more fattally: This comes when it is very Moist and Rainy, in the Spring or Autumn: For then much Water hanging on the Grass (in their feeding) they suck it in, which filling their Flesh with a kind of a Dropsical Watery Humour, which always gets between the Skin and the Flesh, putrefying the Liver, &c. and so causes them to dye of the Rot. To Remedy this, give them Parsley, dryed Hay, and Hare Thistle, lay warm Litter near their Holes, with Boughs over it, to shelter them in at Pleasure, against the Wet and Fogs, or Moist Winds, &c. and renew it as often as it grows Wet or Musty And when the Snow lies on the Ground, shovel and sweep it from their Burrows, that they may come at the Grass. And thus have I briefly shewed you how to manage these profitable Creatures, to keep them in good Case, cause them to breed well, and to be free from the Sickness incident to them, which cannot but prove profitable to one or another of my Readers, tho' not to all.

To keep and order Hares in Warrens, or Tame them in all respect as the Coney.

AS for Hares, if kept Tame, or in Warrens, they may be ordered in all respect as the

Coney,

Coney, they being much of the same Nature, and their Diseases the same; but seeing many are desirous to find them wild in the Field for their sport, and advantage of getting them, and are Ignorant of their haunts, and their forms whereby they lose much labour in a fruitless search, and are often disappointed, I thought it convenient to say something to this particular, a Thing desired of me by so many.

When you go about to find a Hare, that you may not lose your Labour, but be more certain in the Event; if you attempt to do it, go not into the thickest of the Cover, but to be more certain, beat the Bushey close or Shruby Ground adjacent; For if you should find a Hare in a close Woody Cover, you will hardly bring her out to shew you Sport, and consequently lose her, but if you find her in the Shrubs, she will, when started, or Chased, immediately take to the Champion Ground, because a Hare naturally delights not in Cover till she is tired, and therefore the Champion Grounds are the most likely places to find them and run them down, and in such Grounds resort to the Gss, Brakes, low Bramble, or Broom. And if they afford no such shelter, repair to the Stubble at the beginning of Hunting Time, and about *Christmas* to the Fallows, and in *March* to the Green Corn, and in those Places the best Hares Hunt, and are usually to be found, and many times you may find a Form when the hare is absent, or gone abroad a feeding, and if you would know whether she hath sat, or has left it, take these Directions.

To know the New or Old Form, whether Retained by a Hare or left, her Shifts &c

THis is a main point to be Discovered, therefore mark in your Search very narrowly the following Directions, to know it it be New or Old, observe if the Form or Seat be plain and smooth, the Pad before is flat and worn, and the Pricks of his Feet so New and Plain to be Discovered, that the Earth appear Black, or so Newly Broken, that the Hare cannot be long gone, then the Form is new, she is not far from it, nor will delay long returning, unless frighted away by some Accident, but the contrary appearing, it is Old, and it you expect any Advantage by it, you will in all likelihood lose your Labour, and another thing is worthy of Remark, and that is, The Hare has diverse Slights and Shifts to avoid pursuit, as are Windings and Doublings, you must also, when she is persued, observe the Leaps and Skips, before she Squats, and beat the Place most likely to give her shelter, for being reduced to these hard shifts, she is tired, come to her last cast, and can hold out but a little longer, for she never uses them till she finds her Strength so failing her that she grows heartless, and has but this way to hope avoiding the persuers.

To know whether a Coney or Rabit be Old or Young, or New, or Stale kill'd, &c

THis is a Nice Point, and many have been deceived in it, and therefore having treated of these Creatures in other Matters, this as very useful, will be convenient enough to set down in the close of it.

If a Coney be Old, her Claws are very long and rough, and long greyish hairs will stand out amongst the Wool, but young and a right Coney or Rabit, it will have a small grisly knot on the outside of the Foot, a little above the Joynt, the Claws middleing and smooth, and no grey Hairs appearing; pinch the inside of the Belly, and it will break tender, but if it be Old, in pinching it will be rough and ruckle up

If stale killed, it will be limber, the Skin taken off, the Flesh look blewish, and have a kind of a slime upon it, but if new killed it will be stiff, and the Flesh white and dry.

To know whether a Hare be Old or Young, new or stale killed, and whether a Hare or Leveret?

A Hare if new and clean Killed, will have the Flesh of it White and Stiff, but if Stale in many places will be blackish and Limber, if the Cleft of her Lips spread much, and her Claws be blunt, and ragged, she is Old, but if the contrary appears, then she is Young

As for the Leveret, as to her being new or stale Killed, the Marks and Signs are the same with the Hare, but to know whether she be a true Leveret or a Hare, requires another Mark to distinguish it, *viz*, Feel with your Thumb and Finger on the fore Leg, near the Foot, and if there you find a small Knob, or Bone standing out, it is then a true Leveret, but if no such thing appear, then it is a Hare, and if you take it otherways, however it may be vouched to the contrary, you are infallibly imposed on, if you take it for any other than what I have mentioned And thus much for those sort of Creatures, bringing great profit and pleasure to this Nation, more particular than to any other.

The

The Faulconers Choice Instructor, or the best way to Manage, Mew, Feed, Purge, Succour, and keep Hawks to Fly at all Sorts of Game, and to do what ever is Requisite for their Pres-rvation, well Ordering, and to make them Expert in what they are designed for or required to perform.

Of Hawks in General, and what Game they most Properly Fly at.

AS for Hawks, they are properly held to be of two Kinds, the Long and Short Winged, the

the first of these are Comprised in the Ger-Faulcon, Faulcon Gentle, the Sare and Lyner, the Merlin, Hobby, and Barbary Faulcon; the latter in the Goss Hawk, Terril, or Tarcell of the Goss Hawk, the Musket, and Sparrow Hawk.

The Faulcon Gentle is accounted the best, and is indifferently Trained either at the River or Field, for his flight at the Water or Land Fowl, as at the Mallard, Duck, Pheasant, Partridge, *&c.* The Ger Faulcon, is proper for the Heron, the Sare, at the Bittern, or Crane; the Lainer at the Pheasant, Partridge, and such like Birds; the Barbary Faulcon Flies seldom well at any Thing but the Partridge the Hobby and Merlin make their flights at the Partridge, but chiefly at the Lark and other small Birds, the Sparrow Hawk will take the Partridge, Black Bird, Thrush, and other small Birds, the Goss Hawk or Tercell, Flies at the Hare, Pheasant, Partridge, *&c.* The Musket is only proper to Fly at the Bush, and thus much for their Flights. The next thing to be considered, is the well Ordering and Managing them

How to Order Hawks taken from the Cage, &c.

HE that has the Ordering of Hawks from the Cage must Bathe them with Warm Water and Pepper, which will free them from Lice, Nits, or any Vermine they Breed, that hinders their Thriving, then feed them well, that they may grow Lusty, to Oppose incroaching Diseases Incident to them, and then Observe (after every Flight) whether at their proper Prey, the Lure or Train gives the Hawk a Casting, if a long Winged Hawk, Flannel is proper, if short Winged, let it be Plumage, and keep them very sweet and Clean

Clean, then, unless in the Days of Bathing Weather, take the Hawk abroad in the Evening and take Care that you Feed him not on two several Meats at once, and above all, let him have no Salt Meat, nor that which is too Fat.

If you intend to make a Flight in the Field upon the first Springing of the Game, Cast off your Hawk, especially when he has Ready Judgment to prevent the Stealing away of the Prey and his Eyes quick about him to discern the least Motion.

If you intend to make a Flight for Prey at the River, Cast him off before he comes near the Fowl, neither let him see it before he is at his full Pinch, then after the Fowl has been twice or thrice Enewed cross it, and after the Hawk has killed her, give him for Encouragement the Head, Gizard, Heart, Neck, and Legs.

To Manage your Hawk after the best Way, to keep him from sleeping you must frequently carry him upon your Fist, often Stroaking him, and to please him the better, have constantly with you the Wing of a dead Fowl, that he may Tug at it, chear him with your Voice and Looks, and so he will become pleased, and Familiar, and use him in the like Manner to be Acquainted with the Horse and Dogs, so that he may become Bold and Fearless.

How to bring your Hawk to the Lure.

TO bring your Hawk to the Lure, do it by degrees and not hastily, as in the first place, to jump upon your fist, and after that the Lure, then Cherish him with your Voice, and give him something to encourage him, that in time the, be obedient to every call, so that upon the sound of your call, or the sight of the Lure, he may readily comply with your desire, and when he does it, give him some

Part

Part of the Fowl, but if he refuses, Fasting will bring him to Obedience, by abating his Stubborness for self Interest

As for the short winged Hawks, you need but only call them to your Fist, and as for the Lure and Variety of Loud Voice, requisite to the other, it is Indifferent to them, for cherping will bring them to your Fist, and make them familiar and obedient.

The proper time for Lureing is Morning and Evening, when the more to Tempt and Delight him, hang Bloody Meat about the Lure, and when he is perfect at these Things, carry him abroad, the Weather being Fair, and let him Bath himself in some clear Spring, as Deep as will take him to the middle of the Thighs, take off his Hood, and Padling to make him the apter to Sprinkle himself, or you may set a shallow Vessel of Water, covering the bottom with Gravel and Sand, and so it may be done in any Place.

To Enseam Hawks, or otherways Order them: To Enure them t Flight, &c.

TO Enseam your Hawk, take the following Directions, *viz.* Give him two or three bits of Hot Meat in the Morning, but none at Night, and in this Case the flesh of Rooks or Crows is exceeding good, first washed in Water, and every four Days a Hens Neck, washed and Cut, and so Order him till the Pynions of his Wings feel soft, then give him a Casting (as before Directed) and sometimes a live train'd Pidgeon. let him be long and often upon the Wing so that his Grease and Foulness may Dissolve, when this is done.

Take three Pellets of the Roots of Sallendine, an Herb so called, steep them in Syrup of Roses, and let him Swallow them, which will Purge a-

way

way the Foulness and overplus of Grease, Enabling him thereby to be Lively, Nimble, and make a good Flight.

When he is Maned, Lured and Ensnared then is your proper time to bring him to the Flight, which if it happens to be at the Pheasant or Partridge, in Woody or much Inclosed Ground, then upon Lureing him, cast the Lure into some Bush, or low Tree, that you may bring him to a stand, then draw it out, and give him Notice that he may Seize it: Feed him daily on the Ground, under some Shrubs or Bushes.

When you first Fly him at the Game, it must be at such as are Young, the Faster to be taken and Mastered for his Encouragement, but if it be a long winged Hawk you five in Champion Ground, do what you can to keep him from the Stand, and Maintain him on the Wing till you or your Dogs have sprung the Game under him, when having the Advantage of stooping, he may the easier Strike and Subdue it, but if you be for sure Killing, more than for Sport, to Encourage your Hawks, first Spring the Game, and Mark it; which being come to the Mark, cast him off, and when he is got to his Height, lay in your Spannels that so you may Retrieve the Game Underneath him: And after this Rule, with little Variation, long fly all Manner of winged Hawks.

The Management of Hawks in their Flight, and Particularly to Fly at the River

As for short winged Hawks, it will be proper to fly them from the Fist only, and to make them Bold and Couragious, hide a Partridge or such Foul as they take, under a Hat, or some such thing,

thing and when you have well managed the Hawk, let go the Train, and cast off the Hawk, whilst your Spannels are upon the Range

To make the flight at the River, and the Hawk expert at it, Whistle off a Hawk, that has been well Experienced, and is a sure killer; suffering him so long to Enew the Foul, till he bring her to the Plague; then having taken him down, reward him for his Encouragement, then let him by to be ready on Occasion, and Whistle off the Young Hawk and when he is at the Height of his Gaile, and make him (by often shewing it him) Familiar with the Water, and at any time when he Looks out to make him more Inward, Call him with a Gibbet call, and so order him, till you have brought him over the Fowl, and make in, on both sides the Water, where the Game is, with your Company, and lay forth your Fowl, which if the Hawk Strike and Truss, make presently in and helping; so Crossing and Breaking the Wings of the Fowl, that he may secure her, and take his Pleasure of her; but if on the first stoop he kill her, and suffer him again to take his Gail, lay the Fowl forth as you did before, and continue so to do, till it is Landed, then for his Encouragement reward him with the Neck, Gizard, and Heart, but if it happen the first Fowl (by Strength) escape him, flying him immediately on another more Weak, lest, by being baulked, he grow faint hearted, and Bastardly in the Attempt for ever after.

A Plain and Easie Introduction to the most curious Art, and Healthful Exercise of Ringing Musically on 3, 4, 5, 6, 7, 8, or 9 Bells.

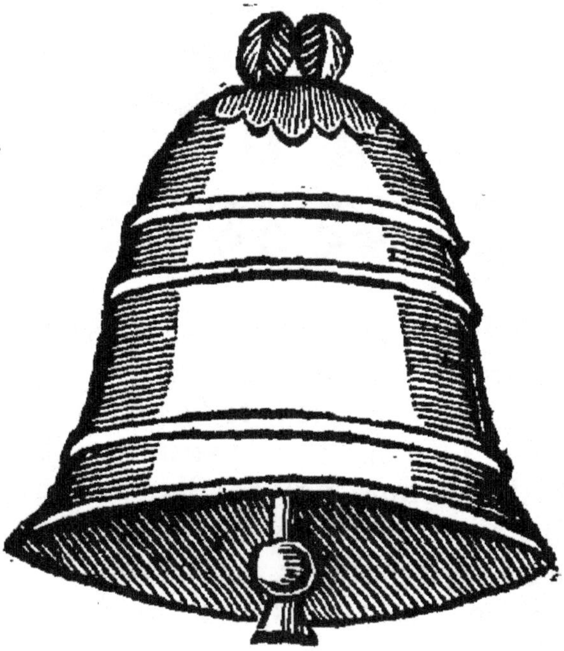

SInce the Knowledge of this Art has been much desired by many, and is a very Healthful as well as Pleasant Exercise, I have placed an Introduction to Young Ringers in this so useful a Book of Rarities, though at first sight it may appear a Digression from the rest; however, since I designed to Work to fit every one as near as may be, I cannot but conclude that this will be desired by many, and cannot be hurtful to none.

The

The Invention of Ringing is Mathematical, producing wonderful Effects, as I ſhall ſhew in the Sequel

Of the Changes

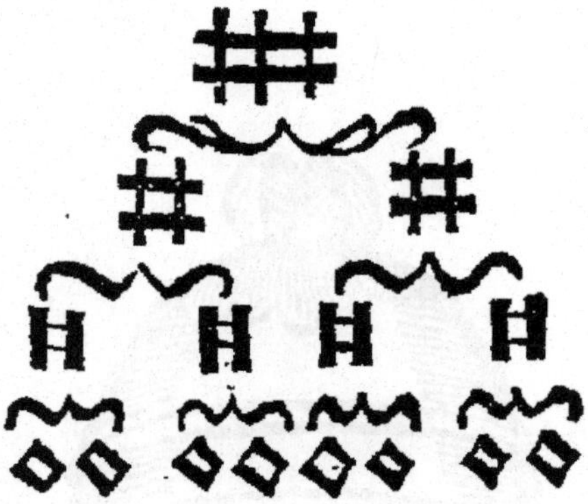

THE Number of Changes are thus to be Ordered, Two muſt firſt be Admitted to be varied two ways, and ſo to find out the Changes in Three, Two muſt be multiplyed by Three, and ſo the Product will be Six, and that multiplyed by four, will produce Twenty Four, which for the Changes of Three, is the compleat Changes on Four, and theſe multiplyed by Five, produce 120 the compleat Changes on Five, and multiply that 120, by Six will produce 720 And that makes the compleat Charges on 6 Bells multiply this 720 by 7 and it produces 5040 And conſequently as the Changes riſe and fall, the Numbers are more or leſs, and may be carried ſo high, that Arithmetick wants a Number to Name them, for an Age is not ſufficient to Ring them out, though every Change ſhall Vary to Admiration

As

As for Example, we admit, the Figure 1. and 2. may be crossed in this manner 1. 2 and then 2. 1 thus allowed, though the Number are never so many as on 3 4 5 6 7 8 or 9 Bells, the same figure thus set down a Thousand times, will Vary particularly on the three latter.

Of Peals.

THE Musicalness of the Changes not being very Intelligab'e to ordinary Ringers, and the best many times Puzled, and at a loss to find them out, the more Judicious Professors concluded it is necessary to cast Peals, that so Musical Notes might the better strike the Fancy, and lead them more sensible and easier to a true understanding in Ringing, rendering it (for their Encouragement) the more taking and delightful, for every Peal on Bells Tuned, to the Principals of Musick, express the Notes, for in a Peal of six Bel's, you have exactly the six Musical Notes. viz *La. Sol. Fa. Mi. Re. Ut.* But to make them charming and harmonious, they must be struck with Skill and deliberation, gradually striking or leading with the lowest Note, and so rising up to the highest, and then down again to the lowest, causing the fourth Bell to Hunt up to the Seventh, and then dodg'd, unless prevented by the Treb'e, and so any other of the number Seven, so that, in the compleat number of Changes of the first striking, there shall not be rung over twice the same. And in this doing, you must have a Musical Ear, and a Steady Hand, to observe the least Defect, and mend it. To

mend

mend or reverse it by dodging, or falling in course, as the Bells hunt up and down, by putting in between, or taking place in a compleat Harmony.

Of Cross Peals

HAving already laid the Ground Work for plain Peals, to introduce the Learner, I now proceed to Cross Peals. These are so Termed, because of their intricacy, or Cross method, wherein diverse Notes moving as it were, at once Cross each other, some moving up, and others down, at the same time, and that the Learner may the easier find it out, and Comply with it, let him observe, that one Note carried the Hunt, is a Guide to the rest, making one constant motion, and uniform throughout the Peals, differing from that of the other Notes, though keeping a continual Motion through the several Notes strucken, *viz* From the leading to the striking behind, and so thence to the Lead; which Motion up and down, is reckoned the compleat Course, tho' some Peals on Five Bells, as the old Doubles, *&c.* Consist only of single Courses, every single Course admitting to Changes; and twelve Courses are a compleat Peal. Other Peals on five Bells, as the *London Paradox*, &c consists of Double Courses, 20 Changes going to every Course, and 6 double Courses to the Peal; but on 6 Bells there are double and single Courses, *viz* 12 Changes in every single Course, as in *Grandsire Bob*, &c. The Changes wherein the Hunt

leaves

leaves leading, is properly the first Changes in every Course, and in Cross Peals all the Courses a gree in three Respects (1) in the motion of the Hunt, (2) in the Motion of the remaining Notes, (3) in making the Changes, which being exactly taken Notice of, may serve as a certain Guide to the rest, some few Changes in each Peal Excepted.

The Example.

IN this Example I present the Learner with a Pea of new Doubles, only on 5 Bells, they beingl

First Course.	Second Course.	Third Course
12345	13524	15432
21354	31542	51423
23145	35124	54132
32415	53214	45312
23451	35241	54321
32541	53421	45231
23514	35412	54213
32154	53142	45123
31245	51324	41532
13254	15342	14523
13524	15432	14253

the 3 first courses of the Peal, wherein observe, that the last change of the first courses, *viz.* 1, 3, 5, 2, 4, is

is

is set down again at the top of the second Course, and likewise the last Change of the second Course, *viz.* 1, 5, 4, 3, 2, takes place to the top of the third Course; so that Note, the lowermost Charges are the ten Changes of each Course, and as to the Motion, properly the first, the Hunt directly moves up behind, were twice lodging, it proceeds down again to lead, and there also lodges twice, as in the 3 Courses is demonstrated, also throughout the Peal, as the second, third, fourth, and fifth Bells move through the first Course, so these Bells that are lodged in the second, third, fourth, and fifth places in the last Change of every Course, moves in like manner, as tho' the next following Course, and by Moving, Change Places, as to the rest not so well to be shewed in Words, or Practice; for you must consider, in every cross Peal the Courses equally agree, *viz.* first in the Motion of the Hunt, secondly in that of the rest of the Notes, and thirdly, in the making the Changes.

Of Doubles and Singles on four Bells.

TO Ring 24 Doubles and Singles on 4 Bells, take Notice the Peal Consists equally of Double and single Changes, the one Change double, and the other single throughout the Peal, the first is the Hunt, to the remaining 3 Extream Bells; the double Change is every time likewise made of the two first, and the two last Bells, every single Change of the two Middle ones, accept when the first leads, and then we term the Bells that are behind, the extreams, All these Bells have direct Hunting Courses up and down, till the first Leads, then whilst the two hinder

most

most make a Dodge, the Second lies still, and by this Method all the Bells proceed again in their Hunting Course, there being after this Manner; Extream Changes made; That is to say, the first every time the Hunt leads; the second, always when it lies behind; and the third, every time it leads, and lies behind.

The Peals called the Old Doubles and Singles on Five Bells.

IN performing this, obſerve that one Change muſt be Double, the next Single, and ſo in their Turns, till the Treble has the Direct Hunting Courſe, as in Caſe of the plain Changes, every Double Change, ſtruck on the four firſt Bells, conſidering the Treble to be One of the Two that makes every ſingle Change, unleſs when it Leads, and when the ſingle is in the Third and Fourth Place; but when the Two Bells lie next to the Treble, you muſt conſider that behind to be the ſingle Bell which is called the Extream; and obſerve, that every time the Treble leaves Leading, the two firſt Bells are to continue Slow Dodging, till it be altered by the coming down of the Treble, which diſplaces them; and the Treble Moving down out of the Fifth Place, the Bell that comes into it muſt Remain Silent, till the Treble Hunts up to it again, except when the Extream Change is made behind, every Bell lies twice together in the Third and Fourth Place, except upon the Trebles Leading, and likewiſe when it hinders them in Hunting.

The Old Trebles and Doubles on Six Bells.

HEre Mark that one Change is Treble, and the other Double, and so in Order, except one Single at the End of every Sixth Change, every Treble Change being made on the Two First, Two Middlemost, and the two Last Bells, and every Double on the four middle Bells except in Case when the Hunts leads, for it must be upon the Four hindermost, the Treble here being the Hunt, making a Direct Hunting Course up and down, as in plain Changes, as likewise must be considered in the Rest, unless when the Treble Leads; and then such Bells as were Hunting up, except that in the second place, makes a Dodge with the next Bell beneath it, and so again proceeds forwards in its Course up, and every individual Bell, that at the same time was Hunting down, makes a Dodge with the next Bell that is above it, and then proceeds downward in its Course; and such a Method carries on the Peal five Courses of the Hunt, which makes 10 Changes. And thus having briefly given you the Ground-Work of Ringing, with a little Variation and Practice you may frame your self to any Sort of Ringing, and carry the Matter as high as you will, upon 7, 8, or 9, Bells, having a Musical Ear, and Stedy Hand, and being Circumspect in what you are about, and marking these that are Expert in it, how they Order the Management of it.

So the Bells sound, oft Reaching distant Ears,
Seems to them as the Music of the Spheares,
For pressing on the Air 'tis Mounted High,

And

And in Rebounding, Ecchos from the Sky,
Harmonious Numbers Tun'd by Airs, that Beat
Upon the Sounds, as they to Hills Retreat,
And so Deceiv'd, they give a Story Birth,
They Heavenly Musick hear, when 'tis from Earth.

How a Country Man may know how much Hay or Corn his Barn will bold before it be put in.

THis has been desired by many, especially upon taking Barns, and Out-Houses, where they desire to know how they will Answer the Stores Designed to be laid up in them, and for their Satisfaction, I have here found out an Easy Way to inform them, if they know ever so little of Arithmetick.

To be Satisfied herein, Multiply the Height to the Beam into the Breadth, and that Product by the Length, the whole Divided by 20, and so the Quotient readily shew the Load to the Beam, and then for the Roof, Multiply half the Depth into the Breadth at the Beam, and that Product by the Length, then Work as before, and adding it to the other, you will soon be satisfied in what you Desire, and those that understand not Figures, may Easily get any Body that does understand it (by this Rule) in a few Minutes, and Inform them to their Satisfaction.

The Measures that ought to be in Cords or Stacks of Wood.

TO Measure Wood for Fuel, Plank, or Timber going to a Load, is Necessary to be known in the Management of Country Affairs, for at one time or other the Honest Country Man cannot but stand in Need of such Knowledge to Advantage him; wherefore I here set down.

A Cord of Wood ought to be 4 Foot Over, 8 Long, and 4 Deep, making in all 128 Cubick Feet.

A Stack of Wood ought to be 3 Feet Over, 3 Deep, and 12 Foot in Length which makes 108 Cubick Feet, and to a Load of Solid Timber there goes 50 Foot, a Cubick-Foot Contains 1728 Inches, a Cubick-Yard, 27 Cubick-Feet, or 46656 Inches.

300 Foot of a Inch Plank, 200 Foot of 3 Inch Plank, 115 Foot of 4 Inch Plank, 400 Foot of One Inch and half Plank, or 600 Foot of 1 Inch, make either of them a Load of Plank, in True Account, &c.

To tell what is a Clock (when the Sun Shine's) by ones Hand.

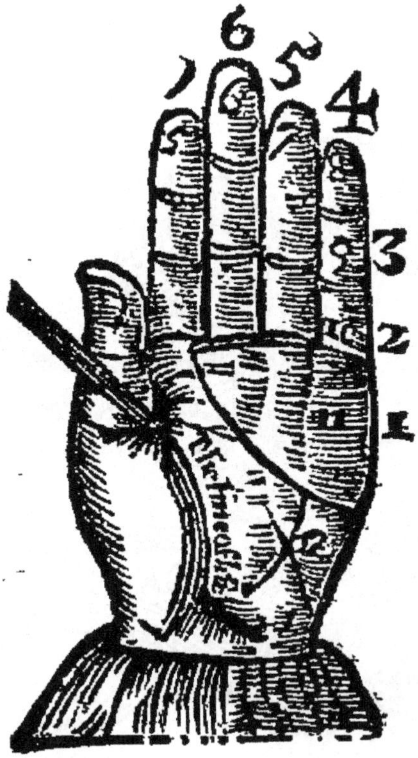

TAke a Small Straight Stick of about Four Inches Long, and hold it between the Fore-Finger and the Thumb, of the Left Hand, and turn about towards the Sun, till the Shadow of the Ball of the Thumb, touch the Line of Life, and then the Shadow of the Stick will appear on that part of the Hand, which tells the Right Hour of the Day, &c. Approved by Mr. *Saunders.*

A Catalogue of the Markets, and the Days they are kept on in the several Countries and Shires in England *and* Wales.

In Middlesex.

AT brainford, tu london m. w. fr. ſa. uxbridge, th. ſtares, ſi. edgware, th. weſtminſter, m w. fr ſa. enfield ſa.

Hertfordſhire.

Barkhamſtead, m. barnet, m. buntingford, m. ware, tu. hitching, tu. watford, tu. richmanſworth, ſa. St. albans, ſa hertford, ſa. ſabsworth, w. hemſtead, th hatfield, th. biſhops-ſtafford, th ſteveednge, ſa. tring, ſa. ſtondon hodsdon, th boldock tu.

Barkſhire.

Reading, ſa. abbington, m and fr wantin, ſa. willingford, tu. and fr. new-windſor, ſa faringdon, tu. newbury, th oakingham, tu. eaſt-eſledg, w. maidenhead, w hungerford, w.

Bedfordſhire.

Tuddington, ſa bedford, tu. and ſa patton, ſa. lutton, m. ſhefford, fr. leighton, tu. bigleworth tu. dunſtable, w. amptil, th woborn, f.

Buckinghamſhire.

Risborough, ſa. great marlow, ſa. oulney, m. amerſham, tu. colebrook, w cheſham, w newport, ſa alesbury, ſa. winſlow, th wendover, th. beconsfield, th. ſtoniſtratford, fr. buckingham, ſa. jvnigo, fr. high-wickham f.

Cambridgſhire.

Ely ſa. new market, tu royſton, w. coxton, tu. linton, th. march, fr. wisbich, ſa. cambridge ſa.

Cornwal Country.

Stratton, tu. penzance, tu. *St.* columb, tu. falmouth, th. market-jew, th *St* Germans, f. gamelford, f. foy, f. listithiel, f. grampound, f. padstow, f. tregonye, f. helstone, f launston, f. bodman, f liskard, truro, w. and f. *St.* Joes w. fr Penrin. w. f f. east looe—faltash—

Cheshire.

Altrincham, f. maxfield, m. Frodsham, w. malpas, m. northwich, f. fambich, th stopford, f. nantwich, f. middlewich, sa. congleto, sa. huntsford, sa. westchester, w. and sa. tarvin.

Cumberland.

Brampton, tu. cockermouth, m. wigton, tu. alley hom, sa. keswick, sa. perith, tu. bottle, w. widthaven, th. ravergeless, sa. egremen, sa. long-worth, th. ashron-moor, sa. carlisle, sa. ireby, th. kirswald, th. longrown, th.

Derbyshire.

Barkwell, m allsreton, m wirksworth, tu. ashborr, sa. Tedersswal w. dronfield, th. derby, fr. chesterfield, sa bosover, fr drawfield.

Devonshire.

Tiverton, tu bedford, tu. ottery, tu. exeter, w. fr. axminster sa plimpton, sa honiton, sa. crediton, sa. colnmpton sa southmoston, sa great torrington sa. holsworth, sa teyesleck, sa morton, sa oakehampton, sa. chidley, sa ashburton, sa plymouth, sa. totness sa. kingsbridge sa barnstable, fr. darthmouth, Colliton, tu. harburly, fr chumleybow, th. dodbrook, w rewton abby, w medbury, th.

Brishoprick of Durham.

Durham, sa darlington, m leneard castle, w. sunderland, fr. bishops, aukland, th. stainthrop.

Dorset-

Dorsetshire.

Cern-abbas, w cranbow, w. crofts-castle, th. abbotsbury, th. sturminster, th dorchester, w. frompton, th. wemborn minister, fr. shaftsbury, w. worham, w. blanford, w. pool, m. and th. weymouth, tu. and fr. melcome regis, tu. and fr. sherbourn, th and ———

Essex.

Eppin, fr. chipping ongar, sa. harwich, tu. maintree, tu. waltham abby, tu billerikey, tu. braintree, w. brentwood, th rumford, w haulsteed, fr. colchester, fr chelmsford, fr thackstead, fr. cogshal, sa. malden, sa walden, sa. hatfield, sa. Dunmore, sa. raleigh, sa barkin, sa. hardon, sa.

Gloucestershire.

Wickware, m. deanmag, m Minchinhampton, tu. prisvick, tu horton, tu. letchlad, tu. marshfield, tu. backley, w campdon, w. tedbury, w. cheltenham, th dursley, th stow on the World, th. chipping sadbury, th. newet, fr fairford, th. newham, tr. tukesbury, w. and sa. stroud, fr. wotton-underedge, fr. leonards standley, sa winchcomb, sa. thombury, sa. cirencester, m. and fr gloucester, sa.

Hampshire.

Bansistoke, w kingsclene, tu alceston, th. ringwood, w. newport, in white isle, w. and sa. portsmouth, th. and sa. winchester, w. and sa. southampton, tu. and fr.

Kent.

Dover, w and sa sandwick, w. and sa. eltham, m. wartham, tu St mary cray, w. lenham, tu. wye, th westram, w lydd, tu. rumney, th. brumley, th. foxton, fr maidstone, th rochester, fr. tunbridge, fr smarden, fr. tenderden, fr woolwich, fr. malinge, sa. milton, sa. gravesend, w. and sa. feversham, w. and sa.

Here-

Herefordshire.

Hereford, w fr. and sa. bromyard, m. lidbury tu. pembridge, tu. kyneton, w. webley, th. ross, th. lemster, fr.

Huntingtonshire.

Toxley, tu. St. ives, m. St. notes, th. ramsey, w. huntington, sa. kimbolton, fr.

Lancashire.

Blackbourn, m. boulton, m cartmill m pounton, m hawkshead, m. hornby, m. rochdale, tu. ormkirk, tu. charley, tu. prescot, tu holsington, w. coln, w. warlnton, w. bury, th. gasting, th. ulverstone, th. lancaster, sa clitheto sa manchester, sa. carlton, sa. liverpool, sa. preston, w. fr and sa. wiggam, m and fr

Leicestershire.

Ashby de la Zouch, sa. hinckley, m. leicester, sa. mountsorrel, m. melton mobury, tu. harborow, tu. bosworth, w. loughborough, tu. hallaton, tu. waltham-would, th lutterworth, th. billesden fr.

Lincolnshire.

Gainbury, tu. sleaford, m barton, m. castor-spisby, m market stanton, m market rason, tu. bulingbrook, tu spalding, tu. alford, tu great grimsby, w. glamford, th binbrock, w. burgh th. market deeping, th. holbich, th. folstinham, th wargby, th naverby, th tattershal, fr lincoln, fr. kirton, sa. thoncaster, sa waynfleet, sa. bourn, sa horncastle, sa grantham, sa denington, sa. stamford, m. and fr. lowthe, w. and sa boston, w. and sa.

Norfolk.

Norwich w fr sa. eastharling tu. foulsham tu castón tu hailstone w. attlebury th. watton w sakingham th. northwelsham th. dis fr. wymondham fr east-dereham fr suesham fr. walsinghrm fr. yarmouth sa higham sa thetford sa swafeham sa sew-backingham sa downham se holt sa burnham mar sa. cromar sa. repham sa. alesham sa worsled sa. sechby every second monday.

Northamptonshire.

Thrampton tu. rothwell m. kinscliff. tu wellingborough w daventry w. brackley w. kettering fr peterborough sa. northampton sa. oundle sa

Northumberland

Newcastle tu. and sa. hexham tu. weldér th. morpeth w. alerwick sa. berwick sa.

Oxfordshire

Tame tu woodstock bampton w chipingnorton w whitney th. henley th. banbury th burford sa burchester fr. deddington sa. watlington sa. oxford w and sa,

Rutlandshire.

Upingham w. okeham sa

Shropshire.

Oswestree m great wenlock m. ludlow m elsimeere tu shipton tu brancon w. stretton th. wim th bishops-castle fr widington th. whitchurch fr. bridgnorth sa shrewsbury w. th. sa. newport sa

Somersetshire.

Chard m somerton m glassenbury m. wivelcom tu pensford tu writon tu north-petherton tu. wincaunton w ilcester w. axebridge th, frownselwood w. St. pethuton th. wellington

ton th. bridgewater th canisham th shipton-mallet fr. dunstar-winton sa. langport sa. yeovil fr. crockhorn sa. Ilminster sa vetches sa. dalverton sa. taunton w. and sa. n. cinty tu. and sa. bristol w. and sa. bath w. and sa. wells w and sa.

Staffordshire

Stow tu. new-castle under line m. pagets browledg tu. betles tu tutbury tu. walsal tu. ridgley tu. pancridg tu breewood tu. leek w. wolverhampton w. Utoxeter w. chickley th. litchfield tu and fr. stadord sa. burton on trent th. cockshall fr

Suffolk.

Woodbridge w needham w biddleston w. haveril w. oxford m hadleigh m mendlesham tu. halsworth tu. lestof w. bury w. stowmarket th. tansdale th. saxmundham th. sowley th. bungy th ikesworth fr. new market th. maiden-hall fr clear fr neyland fr. debenham fr surbury sa. aye sa. tramglingham sa. aldborough sa dunwick sa ipswich w. fr. sa. beckles sa.

Sussex.

Satrel th east-grinstead th brighthelmston th. petworth w stenington w. midhurst th steneing w hastings w. and fr coxfield sa horsham sa lewes sa. chichester sa. arundel w. and sa rye w and sa

Surry.

Southwark m w fr sa rygate tu darking tu farnham tu. croydon sa. kingstone sa. guilford sa.

War-

Warwickshire.

Tamworth, s. henly, m southam, m. sutton-cofield, m. aulcester, tu. symeton, tu. atherstone, tu stratford, th. colshil, w. bromicham, th. coventry, fr. warwick, f shipton, s. nuneaton, s. rugby, s.

Westmoreland.

Ambleside, w. burton, tu burg, w. orten w. kerby isauhdale, th kerby stepuen, f kendale, f appleby, f. fardonlike.---

Wiltshire.

Sundon, m bradford, m swyndon, m calne, tu. ashburn, tu. lavington, w. walton, w. highworth, w. hinton, th. devises, th wooton-basset, th dunstion, f. mersbury, f westbury, f. warminster, s. troubridge, s. chipnam, f malmsbury, marlborough, s. salisbury, tu. and s. creeklad, s.

Worcestershire.

Woreester w f f sturbridge, f. bewdley, s. evesholm, m parshore, tu broomsgreve, tu droitwich, f shipton, f kidderminster, th. upton, th. tenbury, tu.

Yorkshire-East-Ridings.

Hedon, f wigton, w kilham, th. bridlington sa packlington, sa. howder, sa hull, tu and sa. beverly, w. and sa.

West-Ridings.

Selby, m. rotheram, m otley, tu settle, tu. sheffield, tu. barnsby, w knaresborough, w. bradfory, th. halifax, th wetherley, th. wakefield, th fr. leeds, tu. and sa. shipton, sa. boroughbrigs, sa pontefract, sa. tedcaster, th rippon, th. snathe, fr. ripley, fr. tickley, sa. bantry, sa doncaster, f t. sherbone, sa.

North-

North-Ridings.

Gaisborough m tickering m thrusk m beda tu. mashram tu. kerby-moorfields w north-alderton w. abberjorth w scarborough th malton sa yarum th helmly sa. york th. and sa. whitnay sa stokeley sa. richmond sa.

Market-Towns and their Days in Wales.

Brecknockshire.

BRecknock w. and sa bal m. coccowell th. beath m and sa

Anglesey

Nebawry tu bewmaris w,

Aberysthway w. llanbeder tu, cardigan sa, tregeron th.

Carnarvanshire.

Kreekych w, bangor w. newin sa. carnarvan sa. palbely w. alberconway, fr.

Caermardenshire

Llanesly tu. kiduelly tu. llandilmawre tu. newcastle fr llangadock th. caremarden w. and sa. lantharne fr llanyuodissy w. and sa.

Denbighshire.

Wrexham m. and th. ruthen m llantest tu. denbigh w.

Flintshire

St. asaph s. holy-well sa. cairvise tu.

Glamorganshire

Carephilly th. cowbridge th powrise th. birdgends sa. lintrissent fr. neath sa cardriff w. and sa. swany w. glamorgan sa.

Radnorshire

New radnor th. knighton th. prestain sa.

Merionethshire.

Herlech sa. belgle tu. bala sa.

Monmouthshire.

Carelyon th. monmouth sa abergavenny tu. port-pool sa. usk m and fr newport sa.

Montgomeryshire

Machineth m. welshpool m newtowe m. Montgomery th llanvilling th. llanidoles

Pembrokeshire.

Rillgarven w. teuby w. and sa bewbeth w. fishguard fr pembrook sa. newport sa. wiston sa. haverford th. and sa.

Note in this Case, that m stands for monday, tu. for tuesday, w. wednesday, th thursday, fr. friday, sa saturday, and according as they are thus markea, the markets are held.

An

An exact Catalogue of the fixed and moveable Fairs held yearly in England *and* Wales, *the Days and Times of their Continuance. The like for Exactness, never before Published.*

THE Fairs are of two Sort, as to the Times of their being held. Some are fixed to a certain day Others change their Days, or are moveable with the Feasts; therefore, since no exact Account, as we know of, has been hitherto given, we shall Labour to satisfie the Curiosity of those, whose Pleasure or Advantage tends that Way And for those that are fixed, take them, for the more regular way, in their Month.

Fairs in JANUARY.

3 at llanbither 5 at hickford 6 at salisbury 7 at llanginny 6 and 25 at bristol 13 at derby 25 at gravesend and churching ford 13 at llondysle.

Fairs in FEBRUARY.

1 at bromley, lank. 2 at bath ashbourn, brickelsworth, budworth, bricklesfield, beconsfield, farington, godlemew, hedon, leominster, lyn, maidstone, reading the vizes 3 at boxgrove and brinley 14 at feversham and oundley 24 at whitland, upingham, welden, tukesbury, highamferries, henley on thames, froom, bourn, baldock 9 at llandaff. 6 at stafford for 6 days 16 at stafford for horses. 8 at taigaron 28 at chestesfield, at winterbourn the second thursday

day in the Month, and at weldonnorth the first wednesday.

Fairs in MARCH

1 at madrim. 12 at alsom norfol. 13 at mounthow. 20 at ale-bury. 25 at montgomery, malden, St. albans, midhurst, malpus, newcastle, northil. 3 days, northampton, ouabuck, ashwel, sharif, burton, gardian great, chart, huntington, St. john's worst, whiteland, woodstock, walden. 12 at wigbourn, woubourn, wrexham. 13 at wye. 7 at worksep 8 tragarron. 18 sturbridge. 12 strudbury, stopford 3 seavoroke. 25 pvobus 17 partrington 4 orham, second thursday at okehampton. 20 at northmore 24 at llamerchemic 1 at lanlegevellah and langadog. 5 at lancaster 27 at derby 20 at durham bromeyard the thursday before 25 at bromeyard 12 at bodman. 13 at bodwin 4 at bedford 3 at brinwell, brakes. 27 atherstone and backwell.

Fairs in APRIL.

The third thursday in the month at yarmouth. 25 winchcomb. 23 at wilton, woodley, tamworth, and wortham 26 at tenterden. 25 at Uttoxiter. 5 at willingford. 11 and 12 at warminster, sudbury the last thursday and saturday in the month. 21 at aberforth. 25 at iving. 23 at ampthill, ipswich, killborough, lougnor, mevemot, hewdley. brewton, birdstock, bilson, bury-lane. neathampton, nul-

Ley

ley Suff. 12 at aberforth 25 abington 26 at alborough 9 at billingworth 25 at bourn 11 at newport-pagnel 23 at Saint pomps 3 at leek, Staff 2 at north-fleet 13 at orleton 25 at buckingham 27 at bosworth 25 at okeham 30 at beverley 23 at castle-comb 2 at rochford 23 at charing cliff chichester and rileborough 20 at stonehouse-green 22 stafford 23 sadbridgeworth and saphire hatfield 25 sawley 28 at soham at sudbnry the last thursday and saturday in the month, at crilade the third wednesday 25 at cleave in wilts cliff in sussex and colebrook 26 at clare 7 and 25 at derby 25 at dunmow 2 and 3 at epping 13 at englsfield sussex 26 at east-greenstead 23 at gravesend for 4 days 23 at guilford 2 at hitchin 23 at harbin hatfield bish and heningham

Fairs in MAY.

1 at llatrifient louth and andover 3 at arundel abergavenny 3 and 10 at ashburn-peak 16 at llangairange 26 at lenham 1 and 9 at maidstone 6 at amesbury 13 at albrington 3 at merthyr 27 at mortgomery 3 at mourton and merchenleth 1 at *brickhil* and *black-burn* 3 at bala 3 and 25 at broomyard 7 at bath and beverly 9 at mayfield 20 at malmsbury 3 at nuncaton 7 at newton 1 at *black-heath* 13 at blackwell 13 at basa meiing 3 at *bicking-ton* 25 at backburn 1 at chelmsford 3 at clifton 1 at congerton 5 at caxton 7 at orford 1 at oivestry 19 at odehill 1 at perin pembridges philips-norton and pombridge 31 at

at pashor 3 at pouthely 1 at reading rippon radsdale stoke nail and stanstead stow in the old and Wendover 83 at rochester 3 at stafford and streton church 7 at stratford evon the first wednesday at weldon north 2 at worksworth 15 at welch-pool at winterborough the second thursday 3 at wadbridge 6 at wellon 1 at uske and warwick 3 at waltham 8 at whemerly 1 at tuxford 3 at thetford and tidswill from 8 to 25 at tollerwilm downs 7 at thunderly 12 at thork 1 at kimar leighton leicester lexfield lichfield ledbury and linfield 2 at leominster 6 at knighton 3 at chersey chippenham and cowbridge the second friday at charlebury 4 5 and 6 at chatham 4 at chesterfield chappeltrith 23 at crainbrook 3 at denbeigh and darby 5 at derb 1 at enfield hounslow greenstreet fockingham grighowel and haveril hope 11 and 19 at dunstable 4 at foresham 10 at fring 2 at fairford 3 at henningham and Huddersfield 6 at hay 19 and hereford 7 at hanslop and hatesbury.

Fairs in JUNE

11 At newport pagnel 3 at alsbury 23 at gloucester 6 at abbington 11 at newport-knees 29 at grogang lane 22 at St. Albans 11 at bolt 20 at hereford 24 at newbury 22 and 24 ot ashburn 26 at northop 17 at hardstock 11 at oakingham 24 at St anne 17 at highham-ferries 29 at onay 24 at awkidborough and halifax 29 at ashwell 14 at pea-

peasey and horstone 11 at bremel *Nor.* 15 at pershore 24 at hertford 14 at bangor 14 and 29 at peterborough 24 at horsham hurst 28 at hescorn 24 and 28 at St. pombs 16 at bleath, breckn 24 at preston 19 at bridgenorth 29 at hodspon 23 at barret 26 at petersfield holdworth horden and pontstephen 24 at barnwell bedford-bedle boverly bishop castle broomsgrove brecknock bosworth great boughton kingston *War* reading ramford shaftsbury stranstock knotford lower 29 at huderfield iver and sarstrange, 11 at norwill-gate 22 at kinkih and 11 at linbyther 28 at royston 17 at greenstow 22 at shrewsbury 11 at selby 24 at burford 29 at bala senock southam stafford stockworth sudbury buntinstord buckingham boston bramley barhemstead and benington 11 at ledbury llanwist llandibadnor 17 at llangivilling 24 at lancister lincoln ludlow leicester 27 at laddogain the first monday and tuesday at thorn 29 at tring upton and thorock 19 and 20 at thwayte first wednesday at carlisle 25 at castle chichen 1 at chappelfrith 21 at Uffranmerick 24 at warminster wakefield wallingford and warwick 29 at llamorgan llambender leominster and lemister 24 at chester colchester croydon craybrook wenlock, and windsor 9 at maidstone 18 at marchenlenth 6 7 and 8 at milton 11 and 30 at mansfield 11 at wellington 29 at mount sorrel maleborough mansfield westminster witney woodhurst 24 and 29 at wolverhampton. 11 at newborough and newcastle 13 at great newton 24 at york 29 at gardiff 19 derby 22 at durham nort. 23 at derby dogeby 19 and

20

20 at fairford 28 and 29 at garstrange 24 at tarnsham

Fairs in JULY.

2 at rickmanworth 7 at richmond 20 at neath 22 at newark northwich and ponterly 20 at odiham 11 at parmeg 15 at pinchback 20 at ashton underline 23 at cheston and caernarven 25 campden chichester chisbolme aldergam and abbington 7 at albrighton 20 at alferton 25 and 27 at ashwell 69 at chappel-hago 22 at stockbury and stony-stratford 17 at stevenage 7 and 25 at roystone 22 at hocking 25 at revenglass reading rosse 26 at rala largway 2 at smeath sweansey 7 at shelto-sweaten 5 at burton upon trent 7 at brentwood 21 at bernard's- castle battle field and bricklesworth thursday before the 21 at broomyard 20 at betley bowling and olton 7 at denbigh 25 at doncaster 23 at davenet 25 dodly dover erith 7 at emlin 3 at fodrin 28 at fairfax 2 at hungtington 10 at foulness 15 at greenstead 3 at harderst 6 at haveril 7 at havertord west 6 at helden 30 at hatfield 27 at horsham 9 and 10 at ingatestone 25 saint james northampton saint, james london saint james ipswich 17 saint kelms 22 kingston kimbolton ketwick and kidwalley 25 kingstone lisle kirkham 6 lambither llamidals 11 lynd 27 llangvillin leek 25 louth leverpool llandervigan 20 saint marg midhurst 22 maudlin hill melenborough 25 and 2 at molpas 25 mochenbeth 28 meuhemot 22 colchester 21 clean cethero 20 catesby cummock colidg 7 and

and 27 chappel-frith 21 biller cay bridgnorth and broughton 25 buntingford broomsgrove brodoack bromley boston bristow bilson bistower barhamstead baldock 26 bewdley 2 and 5 at congerton 7 at carrington castlem canter the third wednesday at cricklade 25 at shemal cr 30 at stafford 7 at treshevimio and tenbury 20 at teuby 22 at turbury 25 thembley-gre rilbury thrapstone thickham and trowbridge 22 at tiptery 7 at the vizes upingham 20 at uxbridge 2 at wooburn 2 and 5 at weln w. 11 at wanton 25 at wilon 17 at winchcomb 22 at witheral winchester whergrig yadlaid and yarn 7 at weald 25 at walden wigmore wetherby and wigmore-

Fairs in AUGUST.

24 At dover 15 at dunmow and dryfield 10 at differingolwick and doncaster 24 crowland 1 at dunstable 15 and 20 at crobay 15 at cambridge carlisle and cardigan 10 at chotley cudlew and croley lanc. 1 at chepstow 9 at aberlew 4 at dantrey 10 at alchurch 24 at aberconway 15 at saint albens 25 alborough and ashby-de-la-Zouch 28 at ashford 1 at banbury and bath 1 and 10 at bedford 10 and 24 at banbury 10 at brampton 9 at bardney 10 and brainford bodwin and blackmore 12 bolton and blackwell 29 at caerwis 24 at beggers-bush bridge and broomly pag 25 at brecknock 1 at nortewchurch 15 at newin 20 at northmore 10 at newborough 24 at newport-more northampton and rajadarg-

way

way 24 at norwich northiderton newbury nantwich and oxford 10 at owndle 29 at okingham ormskirk 6 at peturburg 15 at preston *Lanc* 1 at rumney 10 at rugby 1 et selby 15 at rosse 1 at selborn and shrewsbury 18 yminch the third thursday at yarmouth 1 at york and yeland at wakefield the third thursday weldon north the first wednesday at winterbourn the second thursday 28 at welshpool 24 and 29 at watford 15 at witeland 10 at weldon waltham weldon warminster weydon and winslow 10 at sedolo and sherburn 15 at stroud swansey and stow 25 sudbury 28 at sturbridge w. 4 at thunderly 1 at thaxsted 10 at torcester 13 at turbury 13 at tollerwilme dows 28 at tuddington and talistang-green 28 at tukesbury 1 at wandebridge wisbich newton *Lanc.* newcastle outer excester saint eedes feversham frint hay hornsea nigworth iver in bucks carmarthern kerwilley llanthissent llarwin loughborough ludford and melling 24 at mortgomery and monmouth 10 at marras and melton mowbray 15 at marleborough 24 at *London* and leominster 10 at farnham foresham todsham *Chesh*, fullea hatlehigh hadley hawkhurst hungerford horncastle kenwilgal kellow and shilgarron 15 at eglesfwisbully and elesitere 24 at farrington 15 at gainsborough godhurst hinklea and huntington 24 at honywood and kiderminster 29 at St. Johns bridge 15 at luton 4 at luton ludow.

Fairs in SEPTEMBER.

8 At streton-church stratford avon smalding

 sturbridge

sturbridge in cambridge shire southwark shyndemreath gilborough haulton hertford huntngton atherstone abbington brewood and beaumaris 8 and 29 at blackbourn 29 at aberforth averconway saint albans ashburn peal hay; heady higworth 24 at avergavenny 21 at saint abegwylly helmsley and holdon 14 at hitsbury hidown and roses 29 at higham ferrias 17 at stopsord 26 at soham 24 25 and 26 at at sudbury 29 at tuddington stonehouse-green selby shelford stow *Lance-* tame torrington and tukesbury 21 at shrewsbury and stafford 8 at turby and tuxford 23 at towcaster 25 at inglest wait 21 at katherine hill and kingston *War.* 29 lancaster laveingham 24 at llanvilling 20 llanvelley 17 at llanidlasse 21 ledbury 8 at llidditsel 29 at hingston on hull kingstead and kingston 21 at knighton 8 at knighton 28 at caremarthen 8 at birry *Lancy.* 14 at barsley 21 at buckingham bedford baldock bradle maid braintree bulwick brikinton 10 and 11 at basing-stoke 29 at balmstock bishop stortford bremingham and buckland 27 at basing stock 1 at utoxeter wakehore waltham weld west-mean whitland 13 at valyley 21 at the vizes 1 at whitehaven 7 at ware 29 at uxbridge weyhill weymer 7 days within woodham ferry 7 at woodbry hill 29 at leicester lianidas lanthangle lochr ludlow 8 and 21 at maiden 14 at mouston 21 at marlborough and midnal 24 and 29 at malton *W.* 29 at marcherbeth 21 at nothampton 13 newton 14 newport and newborough 21 nottingham 3 neathyr 14 at burford 1 at capple sieve 29 at burwell black-heath 8 at cardiff carding and

chatton

chatton 14 at chesterfield 17 at cliffe 29 at charlebury 12 and 29 at canterbury 21 at croydon and chappon 25 and 26 countress court fair 29 at chester chichester crisle and cookermouth 21 at cricklade 24 at woodstock 8 at worseworth and woolpit 11 at wooken 14 at waltham-abby wibley and worton 29 at wendover 11 at wallingford 20 at whethera 8 at draiton dryfield 19 at newbury 14 at denbigh 4 at okeham 13 at orlton 22 at daintry dover the first thursday at okehampton 21 at derby 28 at dolgeth 8 at parthne and poulthely 29 at depping *mark*, 21 at peterborough and at easterland 29 at dean 14 at penhade 5 at prubus 2 and 3 at epping 12 at enfield 23 pancridge in *Staffordshire* 8 at reculver 8 and 13 at rockingham 14 at richmond and rippon 8 at greenstreet 25 at greenstead,

Fairs in OCTOBER

2 At salisbury 9 at ashbourn-peak 6 at haven 13 at aberstow 18 at ashweel 30 at abermals 20 at abrighton 28 at ashby-de-la-Zouch and a bero nway 18 at farringdon 22 at saint friswed in *Oxf* 9 at gainsborough 9 and 11 at hereford 13 at greve end 16 at greys 23 at prestow 31 at powlthelcy 11 at radnor 23 ratsday 31 at rathin 13 at royston 8 and 9 at yarmouth 18 at york 13 at wakefield 28 at warminster warwich 7 wilton newmarket oxford 29 at whemerly 14 at newport in *Mon.* 18 at newcastle 21 newport 16 at newark 8 at pontstephen 13 at draiton 16 at deventre 14 at saint edmunstone 18 at eley 24 25 26 and 27 at elvest

 6 at

6 at saint faiths by *Nor.* 18 at ewell 1 and 8 at banbury 9 at barborough 8 at swansey 1, at sevenock 9 at sagridgworth 13 at hitcham and hednor 3 at boltonmora 13 at s. w on the wold 18 at hatfield 8 at bishops st fford and blyth in *Not.* 18 at henly arden 13 at staunton and stotford 18 at holt 28 at hartford 12 at bolton *for.* 5 at bosworth 18 at barnet 28 at halton 21 and 31 at hokelly 28 at stamford 18 at kidwelly 18 at brickhill and bridgnorth the thursday before the 18 at broomyard 23 and 21 at knotsbury low 9 at throckgras 18 at burton on trent 23 at brickleswortb 8 and 17 at llanibther 13 at tanworth 18 at thirst and tisdale 25 at beverly 12 at llangeves first monday and tuesday at thorn 18 at tidswel 28 at biodern 13 at leighton 18 at rowcaster tunbridge and lowhaden 1 at caster and caxton 5 at chappel frith 21 at lentham 28 at tal samgreen lempster leominster and llanedy 8 at chichester 10 at clift 13 at charing 9 at the vizes 18 at uphaven 4 at saint michaels 13 at marsh field stone and colchester 6 at maidstone and wantage 4 at weld 18 at chainey 13 at marshfield 7 at worksep 13 at windsor 18 at wellenboroug marlow chaleton cliff regis middleway nadhurst wiggam and wrickly 22 at wye 23 and 28 at whitechurch 21 at coventry 31 chelmsford and the second tuesday at marsh

Fairs in NOVEMBER.

1 At kellom bricklesworth montgomery castlemain fairford ludlow swaley 2 at loughborough blechingly bishop-castle buckie and elesmere

mere kingstone on thames wilton maxfield ma field leek 23 at ludlow 6 at andover 10 at aberwi green lenton in *Not* and llanbirber 13 at llani hinary 17 at lincoln 20 at St asfell 11 at aberkernen 29 at ashbourn-peak and lawrest 30 abbington and ampthill 6 and 30 at bedford 6 at brecknock-maling morr n 13 at monmouth and marcherleth 11 at bo ingham 23 at bangor and bwelch 30 at maidenhead maiden bradly baldock bewd'e hoston bedforn 6 at newport-pannel 28 at carlin 11 at newcastle under-line 17 at northampton 13 at chelmsford 30 at collinsborough newbury oswestry petersfield pecores preston cobham cibley 11 at dover 12 at doled 11 13 and 20 at St. edmondsbury 6 and 11 at pembridge 2 at pennibout 30 at enfield 11 at tolkngham 10 at rugby 30 at ross and rochester 9 at fa ford and stanly 23 at froom 13 and 11 at garstrange 11 and 13 at guilford 10 at shaftsbury and sh fnal 30 at greenstead 6 at hertford 11 at skipton 13 carven 17 at spalding harlow and hide 19 at horshim 22 at swa hey 23 at landwich 25 at hedon and hiham ferries 20 at health 6 at trigney in *Lanc.* 30 at harleigh 11 at tieam 15 and 16 at thwayt 20 et ingenstone 13 at tudding-ton 5 at welsh pool 6 at wetshod and wellington 10 at wem 11 at withdrig 13 at wellington 30 at wakefield and warington 2 and 11 at york 6 at lesford in *Lanc.* 3 at care marthen 5 and 23 at ludlow 23 at ketters-cross 30 at kimbolton.

 Fairs

Fairs in DECEMBER.

4 at Atherstome at dolgeth newton and puchely 5 at arundel exeter St. edes cased grantham heningham hethan hornse northwiech in *Ch.* sevenage sqalding walling-ford and woodstock 7 at sandhurst 8 at bew-maris clitheto cardigan kimar leicester mal-pus northampton and whiteland 21 at charl-bury 29 at canterbury 21 at hornbury 22 at llandilawer 29 at royston and salisbury 11 at northampton.

Note, *Where you find Words standing for the beginning of a Country after any Place Named,* as Lanc *for* Lancashire Not *for* Nottingham-shire, *&c. then the Place is in the Country: And this is to distinguish them, there being more of the same Name*

An exact Catalogues of the Moveable Fairs, with their exact Times and Places

AT northampton from christmas to June e-very wednesday monday after twelfth-day at buckingham at bankley three mondays after twelfth day at melton-mowbray and salisbury the tuesday after twelfth-day for horses the thursday after twelfth-day at Lanbury and lutter-worth and for three Weeks every thursday after at litchfield the friday after twelfth-day at newcastle under-line on shrove-monday at

cande

candene in gloucestershire on ash-wednesday and the same day at donstable chichester eaton exeter folkingham litchfield royston tamworth tunbridge on the first thursday in lent at banbury the first monday in lent at abington winchester chichester chersey the first tuesday in le t at bedford

At char'ebryo i michaelmis-day St thomas's day second friday in lent on the third monday in lent at stamford for horses on midlent sunday at odiham saffron walden and stamford the fr day and saturday before the first sunday in lent at hertford the sunday in lent at hexccomb grantham suobury and salisbury.

The tuesday after midlent-sunday at leeminster the monday before lady-day at wisbich kendale and denbigh wednesday before lady-day at dolton thursday before lady-day at yarmouth on St. matthew's-day at cricklade.

The tuesday seven night before palm-sunday St. luke's-day at newmarket the wednesday before palm-thursday at daryton and the thursday before it at landissel

On palm-sunday at leicester newport alesbury wisbich skipton and ponfract on the same at billingsworth lancaster kindale worcester llaundaren the tuesday after at wakefield

The monday before easter at ledbury tuesday before easter and St. barnaby's day at selby.

Monday tuesday and wednesday before easter at marsh the same day at ludlow the thursday before michaelmas the thursday before easter and the thursday before St thomas's day at ketter

 ing.

ing the monday before St john baptist at soham the wednesday in easter week at mass-Gate; monday wednesday and thursday in easter week at sosings on saint peter and saint paul at ridbury.

On the eve and feast of saint peter and saint paul at barkstrange, also on the eve and feast of saint martin

On the monday in easter week, and monday before St. thomas's day at thornbury.

At cateline and l'anvillan on the wednesday before easter, and the wed esday and th rday-day before at willingford, kettering and sudminster

On good friday at burnhill, ampthil, brewerton chari g, berry, erfield, guilford, huntington harsi ld, ipswich melian, loughter nutley, S pom's, sborough and roborough

On e ster mono y at o.ay, buck, dr fie'd and garsborough on tuesday at ashby-de-a zouch, da trs, barlets, dorchester, *Oxen* northstree, hi ch ng, retchford ard saml ich

On e ster mo day at w Lingborough and beverly on friday in easter in derby, the next day a, skipton in *Carven*, The second monday after easter at new malton

Monday, tuesday and wednesday after easter at chucley, and on the wednesday at hereford

At lodness every wednesday after easter, martlemas day, at inglestwit, monday before holy thursday bucklam, all souls day, tuesday after pa tecost.

At bricklesworth, evesham and newcastle under-line, on mo day after low-sunday

At lough in *Lincolnshire* the third sunday after easter.

At beverly englefield *Lanc.* roch in rogation week

On enmore-green the first tuesday in every month.

Green street on tuesday before ascension day

At worbly on asension day and thursday three weeks after.

At ross on ascension day and the thursday after trinity sunday.

On ascension eve at ab-rgelly and darkin.

On ascension day at bread-street in *Kent*, bewmaris bridg nd, brimmingham chappel frith, burton on trent eccleshall chapp l, kinnow, egglestrew, St. ed-s hallaton in *Leicest.* lutterworth, kidderminster middlewich newcastle newbury penhold rone rippon stoppor stratford upon avon sudminster yarnwigg and the vizes.

At burrington and thaxsted the sunday after ascension day.

At shrewsbury the wednesday after and at ruthin the friday after

On whitsun eve at new inn, rats-dale, wisbich, skipton in craven.

On whit sunday at kirk b st phen, cabby, lenham rutsdale ryhill and salsbury.

Whit monday at bromyard kingston and grays tuesdays and wednesdays.

At ormiskirk monday and tuesday in whitsunweek, and on the monday at lambiron chipping, agmondsham appleby amesson bradford brickelsworth burton in *Lanc* chichester cockermouth datterington evesham exeter dyfield linton St ives hearts green rigate owndle midlome fleford salford sittinbourn whitchurch and stockeleer.

On whit-tuesday at canterbury ashby-de-la-zouch elesmere daintree epping leightonbuz. knotford high. louguir lewis llaninthebury midhurst monmouth melton mobray oringstock rochford perith.

On the wednesday in whitsun-week at royston sand-bar pont stepen newark in trent libedon llanbedy and leek.

On thursday the same week at saint austel kingstone and chacklefield.

On the friday at stow at guillin derby and gogshal.

On trinity eve at skippton in craven rowel and pomfract.

On trinity sunday at south haven stockley saint mary auk kemdale rowel

On trinity monday at raleigh houndslow ruilly cresswell waterford usk the vizes spilsby and tunbridge.

On tuesday after radnor and abergaveny and the wednesday after at aberfrow

On the day of corpus christi at sanbury saint anns bishop stretford catewid brimicham hallitan egletrew haligh kidderminster hampstead llanwist llammerchimeth newbury neath saint noets newport in Montgomeryshire stooport prescot and rols.

On the friday after at coventry and chepstow.

On the sunday after at stamford and bolton

The sunday after the third of July at haveril and the sunday fortnight after midsummer at fotheringhay.

On the first sunday after saint bartholomew's day at sampbick and ashford and the thursday before St michaels at kettering the monday after saint mich at laseley saint faiths by norwich saint

michaels

michaels and on the tueſday after ſaliſbury on the thurſday at banbury and the friday before ſimon and jude at litchfield, and on the thurſday before ſaint thomas's day at kettering ſtafford ſaint peter's day.

A Table for reducing Pounds into Shillings, Pence and Farthings, and the contrary.

Pounds.	*Shillings*	*Pence.*	*Farthings.*
1	20	240	960
2	40	480	1920
3	60	720	2880
4	80	906	3840
5	100	1200	4300
6	120	1440	5760
7	140	1680	6720
8	160	1920	7680
9	180	2160	8640
10	200	2460	8600

This Table is eaſie, and wants no Explanation, and turned backwards, it is Farthings into Pence; Pence into Shillings, Shillings into Pounds, which at firſt ſight may be thus computed.

The

The true Value, or Worth of a ſingle Penny: Or, A caution to keep Money. Being a way to live happy in hard times.

IT is the general Complaint and Murmure throughout the Kingdom, of ſcarcity and want of money in theſe hard times, where charity is little regarded, vertue rewarded, or neceſſity reliev'd.

The Intent of this following Story is not directed to ſuch as Swim in the Floods of Plenty, who never knew either the worth, nor the want of a Penny, but to ſuch poor Indigent Souls, as either hath, or are likely to groan under the heavy burthen of pinching Penury, and miſerable Want.

Or to any other that are in a fair way to fall into that experimental Diſeaſe, called, *Conſumption in the Pocket*. That when they get a Penny by their Induſtry and Labour, they may know the true value and worth of it, and by following theſe direction, they may learn to ſave a Penny, or to uſe it to their beſt Advantage: And to that end and purpoſe, it will not be a miſs to let you know, what Poverty is, that you may the more endeavour to avoid and ſhun it.

The Definition of Poverty.

POverty is a want of ſuch neceſſary Things, as belongs to our Lives and States, thro' which we are brought to Miſhap and Miſery.

Perhaps ſome may ſay, or think that they are not likely to be troubled with that wretched Diſeaſe called poverty, But I ſay let them have a care, for

for when a Man is Plagued with Poverty and Sickness, both joyned together, without any succour or easement, then riseth in him an intollerable grief, a fire not able to be quenched, a sorrow without remedy, and tempest full of wrack

But, says another, it is not the spending of a Penny, or two Pence, that will bring a Man to poverty. No, but frequent custom of these small expence, will in a short time rise to a considerable Sum, for one Penny a Day spent comes to One Pound ten Shillings five Pence in the Year: And one Shilling a Day comes to eighteen Pounds and five Shillings in the Year.

So that small expences little regarded without a considerable Income, may in time bring a Man to Ruine, and when your Money is gone, you have nothing to trust to but Friends I confess that a Friend in Court is better than a Penny in the Purse However, 'tis good to have Friends, but it is far better never to have need of them For Misery is ever the Companions of borrowed Money

Not that I would have any Man to be so basely penurious, as many of our miserable Curmudgeons are, there is a great difference betwixt Frugality, and Averice And to let you see the baseness of these scraping Earth worms I will intmact a Story or two, concerning Usurers, as followeth.

A Story of a Usurer.

A Country Tenrant, meeting with his miserable Landlord in the Term Time, did offer him the courtesie of a Pint of Sack. To whom the

the landlord said, be a good Husband, and save one six pence and give me the other, and I will take it as kindly as if you had spent the whole twelve pence.

Another Story of a Usurer.

A Miserable Usurer many Days together at a Cooks in *London*, did agree to have a large Mess of Pottage about Noon, and a draught of Small Beer (if required) and as many cuppings of Bread in his Pottage as he would put in, paying him one Penny a Day, being all the feeding he had: If in the Winter, the benefit of a Fire, and in the Summer a farther allowance of Small Beer, *Porrage John*.

Another

ANother Rich Usurer, who made it his custom every Term to travel to *London* on foot, in Ragged Cloaths who sometimes did beg of the Thieves themselves, was so well known tha at last they took notice of him: and examining his Pockets, they found no great store of Silver, but a great Black-Pudding, in one end whereof his Gold was, The Usurrer pleading Hungar. desir d the Thieves for God's sake, to give it him half again, which being granted, and the Usur r finding it to be the wrong end, he desired them to give him some of the Fat of the other end, to eat with his Lean, no you Rogue (quoth the thieves) you have had your Cut already, you shall not have a crumb more.

But

But to return to our subject, concerning the worth of a penny, you must first understand, that there are so many sorts of Pence, as there are several Countries or Nations. Our English Penny is a Shilling Scotch. In the time of King *Edward* the Fifth, our English Penny being round and unclipped, was to weigh two and thirty Grains of Wheat, taken out of the middlest of the Ear, twenty of these Pence made an ounce, and twelve of these ounces made a pound.

But now to the main, which is the simple worth of a single Penny, Observe as followeth.

The worth of a single Penny.

A Penny bestowed in Charity upon a poor body, shall not want a heavenly reward.

For a Penny you may in the Low-Countries in any market, buy eight several Commodities, as Nuts, Vinegar, Grapes, Onions, Oatmeal, and the like.

For a Penny, you may hear a most eloquent Oration upon our English Kings and Queens if you seriously listen to him that keeps the Monument at *Westminster*.

For want of a Penny to pay a Waterman, you may be forced to go from *Westminster*, about by *London bridge* to *Lambeth*, and may truly say you are weary of walking.

You may have in the Market your penny threefold in the same kind, for you shall have penny-grass, penny-wort, and penny-royal, and all for your Penny.

For a Penny you may see any monster, or Jack-anapes, or those roaring Boys at the Tower, the Lyons.

For a Penny you may have all the News in *England*. And other Countries of Murthers, Floods, Witches, Fires, Tempests, and what not in the weekly News-Books.

For a Penny you may have a Boy to walk your Horse, whilst you go into the House to drink a pot of the best.

For a Penny you may buy a fair Cucumber, but not a Breast of Mutton, except it be multiplied.

For a Penny you may buy Thime, which is precious. Yea, and thrift too, if you be a bad Husband.

For a Penny you may have your Dog worm'd, and so be kept from running mad.

For a Penny, a Hostess, or an Hostler, may buy as much Chalk as will score up Thirty or Forty Pounds, but how to come by the Money let them look to that.

For a Penny a Drunkard may be guarded to his Lodging, if his Head be light and the evening dark.

For a Penny you shall tell what will happen a Year hence (which the Devil can not do) in some Almanack or other.

An hard favour'd and ill bred Wench, made Penny white may (as our times are) prove a gallant Lady.

For a Penny you might have been advanced to that height, that you should have been above the best in the City, yea the Lord Mayor himself, that is the top of St. *Pauls*.

For

For a Penny you may buy a dish of Coffee to quicken your Stomach, and refresh your Spirits

For a Penny you may buy the hardest Book in the World, which at some time or other hath posed the greatest Clarks in the Land. That is a Horn Book. The making of which Book imployeth above thirty trades

In so great an esteem in former times have our English Pence been, that they have been carried to Rome by Cart-loads

For a Penny you may search among the rolls, and withal gave the Master good Satisfaction; I mean in a Baker's Basket

For a Penny a Chamber Maid may buy as much red oaker as will serve seven Years to paint her Cheeks

For a Penny, the monarch in a Free School may provide himself of as many Arms, as will keep all his Rebellious Subjects in Awe.

For a Penny you may walk in one of the fairest Gardens in the City, and have a Nosegay made of the sweetest Flowers to please your Fancy.

For a Penny, you may have that so useful at your Trencher, as will season your Meat for to please your Taste a Month.

For a Penny, you may buy as much Wood of that Tree, which is green all the Year, and beareth red Berries as will cure any Shrews Tongue, if it be too long for her Mouth This is Holy Wand.

A Penny may save the Credit of many, as it

it did of four or five young Scholars in *Cambridge*, who going into the Town to break their Fast with Puddings, having sent to their Colledge for Bread and Beer, the Hostess brought them twelve Puddings boil'd, and finding amongst themselves they had but eleven Pence, they were much troubled about the other penny, not having any Book about them to Pawn for it: quoth one bolder than the rest, *Aaudaces Fortuna Judat* *Fortune favours the Adventurous*, and in biting a piece of the pudding end, by wonderful luck spit out a single Penny that paid for it, which it seems was in the Oatmeal, and so for that time saved their Credits.

For a Penny, you may purchase a Plaice which will satisfie any Reasonable Man, I do not mean a Place of a Hundred a Years, but a Fish called a Plaice

For a Penny, a Man may sqency his thirst in the Heat of Summer, when he is almost ready to choak

For a Penny you may see the mad Crew in *Bedlam*,

If you go into *Black-Friers*, or the *Strand* you may buy twelve Taylors for a Penuy in Cucumber time.

At last of all, for a Penny, any one that hath a mind, may buy a certain parcel of Neck-weed, which will cure them of all Deases That is to say a Halter.

There Conveniences and Benefits, and a Thousand more, which a Man might reckon up, doth in the simple worth of a Penny, therefore what Man so senseless as to spend all that he hath, and to leave himself nothing. Although there are

some

ſome that are ſo profuſed and prodigal, yet on the other ſide as I ſaid before, there are others that are too miſerable covetous and ſcraping, as for example: One at *Priors Thorcey near Swaffham in Norfolk*, made his Man pay a Penny out of his Wages for a Rope he cut, when his Maſter, was hanging himſelf in the Barn

Another in the Spring time, would make Boys climb Trees, and ſearch the Steeples for all the Crows and Daws they could find, which he lived upon while they laſted) to ſave others V.&c. alas, becauſe the Market ſhould not be the better for him.

Now there is a Means and a Moderation to be uſed betwixt the two Extreams, Prodigality, and Miſerableneſs, as it called Frugality, or Thriſt, for a Man may ſpend in a moderate Way, as Occaſion or Reaſon ſhall require, according to the old Proverb, *that a great is will ſpend that ſaves a Shilling*

And there are infinite Ways and Occaſions in Spending bnd Laying out Money, as for Meat Drink, Apparel, and the like, but in husbanding our Money in all theſe there is a great deal of caution and diſcretion to be uſed.

Therefore if you ever intend to keep a Penny in your Purſe, be *Moderate* both in your Expences and Apparel, for Wine, Women, and Pride, will conſume a Man although he had a Mint to ſupply his Expences . Then learn to know the vertue of Frugality, which will teach you to hold your own, and avoid unneceſſary expences

As for your Dyet, it is certain that one Diſh or two of Meat, with a good Stomach for the

the ſauce, will give you more content and continue your Body in Health better than variety of Diſhes.

Curious that noble *Roman*, a Man of marvellous Honeſty, Temperance and Valour. When the Ambaſſadors of the *Sammites* brought him a vaſt Sum of Gold, they found him ſitting by the Fire, and ſeeing Turnips for his Dinner with an Earthen Diſh in his Lap. At which time he gave them this Anſwer. *I had rather Eat on this Diſh, and command over them that have Gold, then be Rich my ſelf*

Such Examples as theſe may teach us to keep a moderation in our Dyet, and to avoid Exceſs.

Now for Apparel what need a Man care for coſtly Garments, or new Faſhions, ſo long as he hath that which is Decent and Warm. Yet I muſt tell you, there is Money to be ſaved in buying of Apparel, if you take the advice of an honeſt Taylor. Perhaps you will ſay, ſuch a one is hard to be found. But I will inſtance in one, and ſo draw to a Concluſion.

A pretty Story of an honeſt Taylor

IN *Cambridge* there dwelt ſome thirty Years ago, one *Godfrey Colton* who was by Trade a Taylor, but a merry Companion with his Taber and Pipe, and for ſinging all manner of Northern Songs, before Nobles and Gentlemen, who much delighted in his Company. Beſides he was Lord of *Sturbridge fair*, and of all the miſorders that was acted there

On a time an old Doctor of the Univerſity brought unto him five Yards of pure fine Scarlet, to make him a Doctors Gown. And withal deſi-

red

red him to save every Thread, to mend a hole if a Moth should eat it. *Godfrey* having measured and found there was enough: Laid it by, Nay, quoth the Doctor, let me see it cut out e'er I go: for though you can play the Knave abroad, I think you are honest at home and at your Work. *GOD* forbid else (quoth *Godfrey*) and that you shall find me for give me but twenty Shillings from you and I will save you forty in the making of your Gown That I will, said the Doctor, with all my Heart With that he gave him two Old Angels out of his Velvet Pouch: which *Godfrey* having put in his Pocket the Doctor desired to know how he would save him forty Shillings: marry quoth *Godfrey*) in good faith Sir, let some other Taylor make it, for if I take it in Hand, I shall utterly spoil it, for I never in all my Life made any of this Fashion,

Now for Conclusion, let me advise the to be a good Husband and thou wilt soon get a Penny to spend, a Penny to Lend, and a Penny for thy Friend forget not my Advice, least (after a long Dinner with Duke *Humphery*) you be fain to take a nap upon a Pennyless Bench only to verifie the old Proverb. *A Fool and his Money is soon parted.*

FINIS.

BOOKS, Printed for Richard Ware.

Written by the late Rev. Mr THOMAS DYCHE.

1. DYCHE's *Guide to the* English *Tongue. In Two Parts. The First, proper for Begginners; shewing a natural and easy Method to pronounce and express both common Words and prop r Names; in which particular Care is had to shew the Accent for preventing vitious Pronunciation. The Second for such as are advanced to some Ripeness of Judgment; containing Observations on the Sounds of Letters and Dipthongs, Rules for the true Divisions of Syllables, and the Use of Capitals, St ps and Marks, with large Tables of Abbreviations and Distinction of Words, and several Alphabets of Copies for young Writers. The 20th Edition. Price* 1 s. issued 1729

2. *The Spelling Dictionary: Or, A Collection of all th common Words in the* English *Tongue The Third Edition. Price* 1 s. 6 *d. or both bound together* 2 s 6 *d.*

3. *The Fables of* Phædrus *(who was made a Denizon of* Rome *by* Augustus Cæsar*) under the following Heads, viz* The Weakest goes to the Wall, Chuse the least Evil, Be content in your Station, All covet all loose; Keep not too great Company, &c *Rendered into familiar* English. *The Second Edition. Price* 1 s

4. *The Youth's Guide to the* Latin *Tongue, or, An Explication of* Propria quæ Maribus, Quæ Genus, *and* As in Præsenti; *wherein the Rules are made plain and easy to the Capacity of young Learners. The Third Edition. Price* 1 s.

Just Publish'd.

1. THE Fourth Edition, Corrected of an Introduction to Spelling and Reading English: Being the most plain and easy Method of teaching Young Children to Read: Containing, 1 Tables of Monsyllables, Adapted to the Capacities of the Young'st Children. 2. Tables of Dyssables. 3. Tables of Tryssyllables, with their proper Divisions and Accents. To which are added, One hundred and eighty Lessons, in Words, of One, Two, and Three Syllables, Ranged in Order; and a Catechetical Discourse, Explaining the Rules for Spelling, Pointing, &c. Recommended by many Schoolmasters, as the most practicall performance of its kind, By William Markham. Price bound One Shilling.

2. The Youth's Assistant in the Art of Numbering, being an easy Method of Arithmetick in all its Parts, Vulgar and Decimal. Wherein the young Scholar is instructed in all the Rules contained in the most valuable Science, in a very succinct, but plain and familiar Manner, illustrated with various Examples. Drawn up and design'd for the Use of Schools, with the Approbation of many Schoolmasters, and Persons skill'd in Numbers. By William Markham, Schoolmaster. Price stitch'd 6 d

3. The SYREN, Containing a Collection of 420 of the most Celebrated English and Scotch Songs. Price 2 s

4 Morelands Vade Mecum, or the necessary Pocket Companion, being a book of Accounts ready cast up: Whereby the greatest Stranger to Arithmetick may find the Price of any Commodity from

one

one Farthing to 20 s. with several Tables of Interest; and an Account of all the Markets and Fairs in England, with several other Things highly necessary for all Merchants, Tradesmen and others. Price bound 2 s.

5. New Remarks of London Containing an exact Account of all the Streets, Courts, Lanes, Allys Yards Rows, Rents Squares, &c and where Situated, with a Description of all the Parishes in London and how far there bounds Extend. Also a particular Account of all the Stage Coaches and Carriers, shewing the Days when they go out of Town, and from what Inns. Price bound 2 s 6 d.

6 A new View and Observations on the Ancient and present State of London and Westminster: Shewing the Foundations Walls, Gates Bridges, Churches &c. Also Historical Remarks thereon, with an Account of the most remarkable Accidents, as to Wars, Plagues Fires, &c which have happened for near 1400 Years past brought down to the present Time, Illustrated with Cuts of the most considerable Matters, with the Arms of the Sixty six Companies of London, and the Time of their Incorporation By Robert Burton, Author of the Wars in England History of Popery, &c. Price 2 s. 6 d

7. The Youth's Guide to the Latin Tongue: Or, An Explication of Lilly's Grammer, wherein the Rules are made plain and easy to the Capacity of young Learners by a new Verbal Translation, the Examples declined and the Sense illustrated with Useful Notes and Observations from the best Grammarians By Tho. Dyche, Master of the Free School at Stratford. Price 1 s.

CPSIA information can be obtained
at www.ICGtesting.com
Printed in the USA
BVOW11s2011260117
474583BV00005B/64/P

9 781170 816981